RAILWAYS OF EAST ANGLIA

A History

RAILWAYS OF EAST ANGLIA

A History

OLIVER DENSHAM

THE CROWOOD PRESS

First published in 2022 by
The Crowood Press Ltd
Ramsbury, Marlborough
Wiltshire SN8 2HR

enquiries@crowood.com

www.crowood.com

British Library Cataloguing-in-Publication Data
A catalogue record for this book is available from the British Library.

ISBN 978 0 7198 4033 3

Railways of East Anglia image credits
Alan Taylor Collection, pages 9, 27 (bottom), 43, 54, 55, 56, 57, 60, 66, 79 (top), 80, 81, 86 (top), 92, 97 (top), 99 (top and bottom), 101 (bottom), 103, 104, 107 (bottom), 109, 110, 127 (bottom), 129 (top), 133, 136, 146 (top); Andrew Harvey-Adams, pages 112, 115 (bottom), 117, 118, 119; Arne Hückelheim, page 14 (right); Author (own work or collection), pages 8, 10, 14 (left), 24, 26 (bottom), 41, 62 (bottom), 69 (bottom), 77 (top), 82, 91, 96, 105 (left and right), 134 (top and bottom), 141, 147, 153; British Library, page 12; Cambridgeshire Collection, Cambridge Central Library, page 93; Canvey Community Archive, pages 16, 17; Colne Valley Railway Preservation Ltd, page 145 (left and right); Colonel Stephens Society, page 79 (bottom); East Anglian Railway Museum, page 148; Ian Dinmore, www.railarchive.org.uk, pages 23, 33 (top), 34, 69 (top), 71 (top), 72, 73, 85, 107 (top), 111, 126, 132; Lawrie Rose/Mid-Suffolk Light Railway, page 150; Mersea Museum/Cedric Gurton Collection, pages 129 (bottom), 130, 131; NBE/Southwold Railway Trust, page 140 (left); Peter Treloar Collection, courtesy Lightmoor Press, pages 77 (bottom), 78 (top and bottom); Rev. Simon Pitcher Collection, pages 86 (bottom), 97 (bottom), 101 (top), 106, 127 (top), 128; Richard Allen, pages 113, 115 (top), 116, 120, 121; Simon Nuttall, CycleStreets.net, pages 122 (top and bottom), 123; Southwold Railway Trust, pages 53, 88, 100, 138, 139, 140 (right); Timothy Saunders, page 90; W.J. Naunton/Alan Taylor Collection, page 6; W.J. Naunton, courtesy R.J. Addison, page 137; www.tournorfolk.co.uk, page 143 (top and bottom), 146 (bottom), 149, 151, 152, 154.

Typeset by Simon and Sons

Cover design by Maggie Mellett

Printed and bound in India by Replika Press Pvt. Ltd.

Contents

Introduction

For anyone embarking on their first book, it would be sound advice to avoid opting for too broad a topic – a narrow field that offers plenty of depth is preferable. Sadly I have completely failed to take this sound concept into consideration.

East Anglia is a large region, even when reduced to its logical minimum of four counties, and as with other parts of the country, its railway history has been a convoluted one. Most of the companies mentioned in these pages could justify a book of their own, and in many cases already boast at least one title devoted to their individual histories. In writing this book I have attempted to give an overview of East Anglian railway development, beginning with the early tramroads of Essex and continuing up until the present day (and even into the near future); this results in the condensation of 218 years of reasonably linear development into a relatively small space. Naturally this requires painting with a rather broad brush, but I would hope that this book provides a worthy introduction to the topic, as well as being an entertaining read into the bargain.

Naturally I must offer thanks to those who, in one way or another, have been of assistance to me whilst writing this book. Charlotte Clark of Suffolk Libraries deserves special mention for sourcing a veritable mountain of excellent resource material, more in fact than I could ever hope to process or indeed carry. Likewise the staff of the Lowestoft branch of the Suffolk Archives are to be complimented on their friendly and helpful assistance. The Crowood Press deserves acknowledgement for having sufficient confidence to allow me to write the book in the first place.

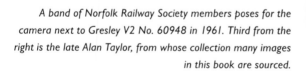

A band of Norfolk Railway Society members poses for the camera next to Gresley V2 No. 60948 in 1961. Third from the right is the late Alan Taylor, from whose collection many images in this book are sourced.

Both Simon MacDowall and Dominic Knight are to be thanked for giving me genuinely useful guidance regarding writing, and Lindsay and Christina Clubb for allowing a complete stranger to photograph their home – whilst Andrew Martin deserves the blame for encouraging me to write in the first place.

Final credit must, of course, go to my family, who have not only given encouragement throughout, but have also listened to more tedious unsolicited railway facts over the past year and a half than any mortal being should ever be required to do. Their sacrifice has not gone unnoticed.

I have tried wherever possible to draw information from more than one source, and to make sure that the information in this book is, indeed, accurate. Any errors or misattributions are therefore regrettable, and as such are entirely my own.

Oliver Densham,
5 April 2021

CHAPTER I

East Anglia Before the Railways

East Anglia is composed of four English counties, which together form a characteristic bulge that swells out from the east coast of the mainland of Britain into the waters of the North Sea. As a result, a long and attractive coastline makes up the bulk of the region's northern and eastern boundaries, affording East Anglia a rich seafaring tradition and fishing industry, and giving many of the coastal

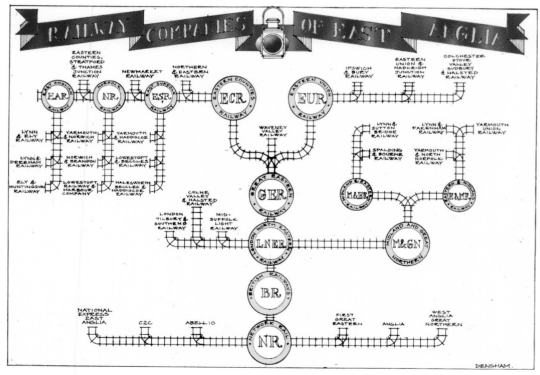

Railway companies of East Anglia.

towns a thriving tourist trade in the summer months. To the south, the region is bounded by the River Thames as it carves its path from the coast to the capital, while the western inland boundary is defined more by convention than actual topography, with the counties of Hertfordshire, Bedfordshire and Lincolnshire grouped along the westward fringes.

Ancient History

Norfolk and Suffolk were the first counties to collectively make up East Anglia, these two being home respectively to the ancient Briton 'North Folk' and 'South Folk', settled tribes of the Iceni resident in the area at the time of Caesar's arrival in Britain in 55BC. Initially pragmatic enough to ally themselves with the Roman Empire, they were later to be led, along with the Trinovantes, in rebellion by Boadicea (or Boudicca, or Buduica, according to taste) around AD60, an enterprise that did not go particularly well.

The residence of the Iceni has left its mark in some of the placenames of Suffolk and Norfolk, including that of King's Lynn (*Lean* being a Brittonic term for an agricultural holding), and more literally in the name of the small Suffolk village of Iken.

The reign of the Iceni did not, however, survive the sixth-century invasion of the Anglo-Saxons,

Britannia Class 70037 Hereward the Wake *at Audley End Junction in the 1950s. Hereward was an Anglo-Saxon nobleman from the Cambridgeshire Fens, remembered for his role in the rebellion against the Norman Conquest.*

The Three Crowns

The Kingdom of East Anglia is heraldically represented by three crowns, a device that inspired M.R. James' unsettling ghost story, *A Warning to the Curious*. Set in Aldeburgh, Suffolk, the story was adapted for television by the BBC in 1972, transferring the location to the Norfolk coastline around Holkham and Wells-Next-The-Sea, with the all-important railway shots filmed on the preserved North Norfolk Railway at Weyborne.

and it is from the Angles that East Anglia derives its modern name. An independent kingdom under the Anglo-Saxons, the region was ruled by the pleasingly named Wuffingas dynasty, named for King Wuffa, who despite having an entire dynasty named after him, may or may not have existed.

Raedwald became the first East Anglian king not born a Wuffinga, and was also the first Christian king of East Anglia. His burial site at Sutton Hoo, close to the River Deben, was discovered in 1936 and yielded a rich harvest of artefacts of high quality, some of which are to be seen in the British Museum, with others on display at the exhibition hall built on the site in 2001.

The last king to wear the crown of East Anglia was Saint Edmund, king and martyr, whose reign ended with the arrival of the Viking hordes in AD869; the Vikings defeated Edmund in his attempts to expel them from the region, and killed him by tying him to a tree and shooting him with arrows. According to legend, the Danes then cut off his head and abandoned it – for reasons presumably best known to themselves – in the woods, where it lay until it was conveniently pointed out to his supporters by a ghostly wolf, allowing it to be recovered and reunited with the rest of him. He was buried, predictably enough, at Bury St Edmunds, although his remains were moved to a safer location in France during the Dissolution of the Monasteries.

Ultimately East Anglia became an area that can be generally defined by the amalgamation of the four counties of Suffolk, Norfolk, Cambridgeshire and Essex. Whilst it was not perhaps quite as flat as Nöel Coward suggested, it has a landscape of gentle character and subtlety, which included large areas of wetland and fen until large expanses of the latter were reclaimed through extensive reclamation programmes starting in the seventeenth century.

Of all the cities in the region, Norwich in Norfolk is the largest, established by the Iceni in the fifth century. Commercially powerful, the city thrived on the wool trade, and was, barring London, England's biggest city up until the eighteenth century, at which point growing industrialization elsewhere in the country led to a slow decline in Norwich's fortunes.

In Cambridgeshire, the cities of Cambridge and Peterborough command the greatest significance,

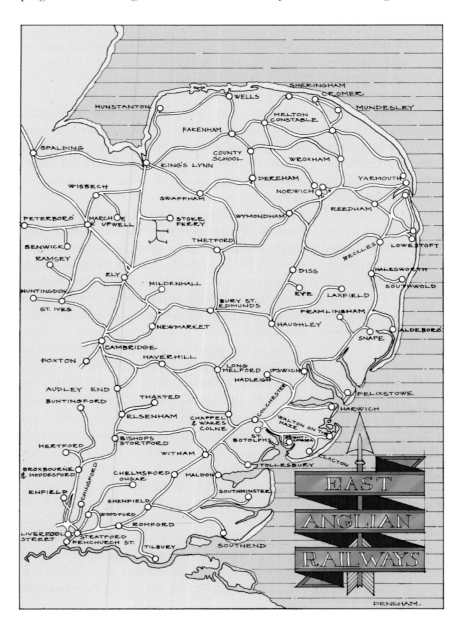

Map of East Anglian Railways, c. 1921.

the ancient city of Cambridge having been the site of prehistoric settlement as well as Iron Age communities from the first century BC. As well as being an early centre of academia, the city thrived on trade links, which grew exponentially with the arrival of the Vikings in the year 875. This role as a trading centre continued even into the nineteenth century, meaning that, unlike Norwich, Cambridge continued to prosper as the Industrial Revolution dramatically altered the economic framework of the country. Peterborough, in its turn, stands out as a city with greater ties to industry, particularly its long tradition of brickmaking. A city located on the Cambridgeshire Fens, Peterborough proper owes its establishment to the foundation of a monastery there in 655.

Ipswich, in Suffolk, can trace its roots back to the Anglo-Saxons, developing as an important port with strong trade links with the Baltic. Ipswich also has a long tradition in brewing, the Cobbold Brewery commencing business in 1746. The name of Cobbold, it should be noted, is one that will appear frequently in these pages. Bury St Edmunds, too, has a strong brewing connection, being home to the Greene King Brewery. The town can trace its history back to AD633 and the construction of a monastery that would grow to become one of the richest religious establishments in the country before the Dissolution. More recently the town boasts a major employer in the form of the Silver Spoon Sugar Refinery, built in 1921.

Moving to the county of Essex, Colchester is widely believed to be Britain's oldest recorded town, reference to its original Celtic name being traced as far back as 20BC. The Romans established a garrison there, and the town has retained its military connections ever since. In mediaeval times Colchester became known as a centre for the weaving industry, and even boasts of its own earthquake, which took place in 1884. Modern-day Colchester, by virtue of its good rail and road connections with London, has become something of a centre for commuter living.

Pre-Railway Transport in East Anglia

In an age of instant communication on a global scale, and liberated by freely available, mechanized personal transport, it is difficult for us to understand the impact that the early railways had on the communities they served. Prior to the noisy advent of the steam locomotive, the fastest mode of land transport was offered by the horse, whilst inland navigation was the only feasible option for bulk transportation, the progression of which could be easily outstripped at a comfortable walking pace.

Stage- and Mailcoaches

For long-haul journeys the only practical solution (disregarding those whose financial position enabled them to maintain their own coach and team of horses) was the stagecoach, services of timetabled coaches drawn along established routes for the convenience of fare-paying passengers, a system that appears to have been established *circa* 1610.

Thus began a tradition that was to last some 200 years on the roads of Britain, but even with improvements in both vehicles and road surfaces, the capabilities of the horses set the upper limit. Speeds between 5 and 10mph (8–16km/h) meant that journeys between major cities would often be measured in days, and a network of coaching inns spread over the country's highways to serve the dual tasks of supplying fresh beasts to replace the exhausted teams of horses, and offering food and accommodation to the passengers. Conditions en route could be cramped, uncomfortable and exhausting, not to mention intolerably cold in the winter months.

The stagecoach routes generally radiated outwards across the country like the spokes of a wheel, with London forming the hub. By 1750, East Anglia could claim a number of stagecoach services, with Chelmsford, Ipswich, Norwich, Cambridge and King's Lynn all being connected to the capital. At that time, the journey by stage between Cambridge and London was timetabled to take two days.

Many of these coaches bore names, some of which have passed down into modern parlance on the mastheads of newspapers – such as *The Times* or *The Courier* – underlining the role that the stages had in bringing the news from one location to another. Others were more colourful but less durable: the London–Boston coach, which passed through

Cambridgeshire via Huntingdon and Peterborough, was known as *Perseverance*, whilst that to Hatfield was *Sovereign*. London to Hitchin was the stamping ground of *Kershaw's Safety Coach*. Since all of the above offered roughly twice the number of seats outside as they did inside, safety (on the roads of the day) must have been by all accounts a relative term.

A further development of the system was that of the mail coaches, conceived in 1782 by John Palmer for the post office. Prior to this date the mail had been carried by relays of men on horseback travelling from 'post' to 'post' – hence the name. These individuals were highly vulnerable to attack, and the whole system simply took too long. By 1784 four routes were up and running, Norwich becoming one of the first cities in the country to receive its mail in this way. The coaches were a significant improvement over the old system, and soon spread throughout the country, achieving impressive (for the era) journey times.

Much of the perceived romance surrounding the stagecoach era stems from its twilight years – the coming of the railways broke the coaching trade's dominion with such speed, comfort and capacity that the old ways simply could not compete. The fickleness of human nature is such that at this point, many of the discomforts and inconveniences of the old stage routes were quietly forgotten in favour of a nostalgic memory of rubicund landlords, glossy horses and bright spring mornings that seemed less harsh and impersonal than the modern, noisy, smoky railroads striding across the countryside. It was ever thus, and as railways began to close in the 1950s and 1960s, displaced in their turn by the car and the new motorways, the railways took their turn in the sentimental limelight.

Inland Navigation

The turnpikes and coaches were of less use when it came to transporting material in bulk. Moving heavy materials was a slow and expensive process by road, the upkeep of heavy horses and the limited loads they could haul meaning that prices per ton were high, and rose disproportionately with each mile thus travelled, impacting heavily on the profitability of any material carried.

Transporting such loads by water brought far greater efficiency in terms of cost per ton per mile, albeit at a pace even slower than that of road haulage. In his short paper *Navigable waterways and the economy of England and Wales*, Max Satchell describes the transportation of a load of chalk marl from Thorpe (Norwich) to Woodbastwick, a distance of roughly eight miles. Rather than transport it by road, it was found to be cheaper to ship the marl down to Yarmouth on the River Yare, a distance of some 21 miles (34km), then back *up* the River Bure to Woodbastwick for a similar distance.

It should be noted that the waterways mentioned above are both naturally occurring rivers, rather than man-made canals. This was the case for many navigations in East Anglia, the natural waterways being 'improved' for navigation purposes, rather than embracing the wholesale construction of canals proper so characteristic of the industrial areas in the midlands and to the north of the country. Even as late as 1835, when the inland navigation system was beginning its slow decline in the face of competition from the new railways, there was a notable dearth of useful waterways towards the centre of East Anglia; as an example, all goods to or from London had to travel by sea around the bulging coastline of the region to or from the mouth of the Thames – no inland route existed from the capital.

Doubtless this had much to do with the agricultural character of the region – had mineral deposits worthy of exploitation been present in any quantity,

Norfolk wherry, captured on the Broads in 1892 by John Payne Jennings.

a more extensive network of canals would have been built up. Nonetheless, such waterways as there were did sterling work for many years, and evidence of them can still be seen today: the Maltings at Snape on the River Alde still retains its quay, and with a little imagination one can still perceive the extensive facilities at Halesworth, where further maltings buildings still stand, and Quay Street retains many of the buildings associated with a thriving and prosperous quayside. (A few hundred yards away at the top of the hill behind the old maltings is Halesworth station, which should give a clue as to where all *that* traffic went to.)

Rather than the characteristic narrowboats associated with canal traffic, East Anglians would become familiar with sailing lighters, trading wherries and Thames estuary barges, the latter capable of undertaking the sea journey around the coast from the Thames to the inlets of the East Anglian rivers.

The problem, as ever, was that of getting the goods from the quayside to wherever they needed to be. Not everywhere was within reach of a navigable waterway, and the prices of certain goods could still be high after road transport from the quayside. Coal was a significant case, and the price of coal in the early nineteenth century was a major factor in the development of industry. What was needed was a form of transport that was not only efficient, but also *fast* – and flexible enough to reach a far wider number of inland locations than could ever be possible with the waterway network.

The First Railways

In the north of the country, the early development of railways as a faster and far more flexible alternative to inland navigation was driven by the pace of industrial growth, which in its turn was driven by the rich mineral deposits and raw materials that were locally available. In the north of England, iron plateways were already a familiar sight in the eighteenth century, whilst even before the dawn of the nineteenth century there were those who were turning their imagination towards the transformation of the huge, inefficient stationary steam engines

of Thomas Newcomen and James Watt into compact, powerful machines that just might be able to propel themselves along the iron road and perhaps even outperform the horse. In fact, had it not been for the restrictive patents of Boulton & Watt and their litigious enforcement of the same, the world might have seen the first steam locomotive set upon rails before the eighteenth century had passed.

In East Anglia, however, matters were different. The region was almost exclusively agricultural, with few mineral deposits to be exploited within the four counties, and very little industry compared with other parts of the country. The population was quite thinly spread, the east of England being characterized by relatively small settlements, market towns and villages whose commercial enterprises were restricted to supplying the wants of a local agricultural population. Beyond the typical red brick, flint and clay tile of the region, the bulk of raw material for any industrial activity, such as coal, minerals or iron, had to be brought in by sea.

Whilst there were some early isolated implementations of rail transport to the south-west of the county in the earliest years, as will be explained in this chapter, the rural nature of East Anglia did not initially provide a fertile environment for the growth of that new phenomenon, the iron road. The nature of its commercial prospects, unlike those of the north, meant that the demand for flexible forms of heavy transportation simply did not exist, whilst the raw materials for the development of such technology were not native to the area.

On reflection, this seems something of a chicken-and-egg situation – industry simply could not flourish in such a region unless the railway facilitated its growth, and the lack of that self-same industry meant that the driving force that was behind the growth of the railways in other parts of the country was simply absent. Furthermore, it would seem evident in retrospect that the railway would be of considerable benefit to a region with a far-flung population – although it should be borne in mind that in the early years of the nineteenth century, the railway was not perceived primarily as a form of transport for people. The early railway was an industrial and commercial tool, and it was only later that the benefit of conveying passengers was realized and exploited.

Horse Tram-Roads

Prior to beginning the research for this chapter, I had assumed that the story of rail transport in East Anglia would begin with the incorporation of the Eastern Counties Railway by Act of Parliament in 1836. In fact the narrative starts much earlier. Notwithstanding the arguably fraudulent promotion of the Norfolk and Suffolk Rail-Road Company in 1824, to be discussed later in this chapter, the appearance of mineral tram-roads in parts of Essex can be traced back to 1805, representing an early adoption of the technology for this predominantly rural area.

Mineral tram-roads, by which is meant primitive iron railways or plateways, were a familiar sight in the industrial North East in the seventeenth and eighteenth centuries. They reduced the rolling resistance of laden vehicles through the use of a low friction interface between an iron wheel and an iron rail, meaning that over an established route, far greater tonnages could be moved easily by a single horse. In this regard the tram-roads of Essex, built early in the nineteenth century, were latecomers to the table. However, to put them in a wider context, only two years before, in 1803, Cornish engineer Richard Trevithick set the world's first steam locomotive successfully on the rails of the Pen-Y-Darren tramway in Wales, laying the foundations for the Railway Age that would change the face of industry in the latter part of the century.

Three significant tram-roads were built in Essex, the first being that constructed by a Mr Whitbread

in 1805, to serve his chalk quarry at Purfleet, on the banks of the Thames. It utilized iron rails, which at this time would have been cast, rather than wrought iron, laid to a gauge of 3ft 6in and which, according to contemporary reports, increased sixfold the amount of material that could be moved by a single horse. Quite a technological novelty in the region at that time, it is described as effecting a reduction in the number of beasts fully employed in haulage from a stable of twenty-five to a mere four, with a commensurate saving in cost – an archetype for the many similar systems that sprang up in quarrying or mining districts elsewhere all over the country.

Typically in their turn, the more established systems would evolve further into fully fledged railways, although there were many (albeit truncated) systems operating in Wales and Shropshire that hung on to horse haulage well into the 1950s, before being finally replaced by road transport.

The Cheshunt Monorail

Mr Whitbread's tram-road was considered noteworthy at the time, but perhaps not quite as noteworthy as the venture of Henry Palmer at Cheshunt, serving a brick and tile works in the Lea Valley. Engaged by individuals who were either exceptionally far-sighted or possibly just easily misled, Palmer had worked under the great canal engineer Thomas Telford before achieving eminence in his own right as an engineer and founder member of the Institution of Civil Engineers in 1818.

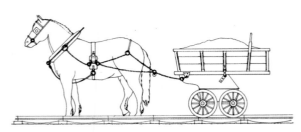

Horse-drawn Purfleet wagon.

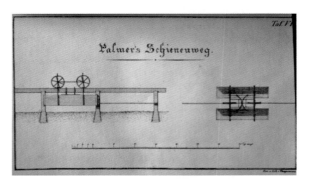

The first monorail in Essex – contemporary drawing of Henry Palmer's monorail.

Curiously, since he will appear again in these pages, Palmer had campaigned strongly against the Liverpool and Manchester Railway in favour of canal interests, but at Cheshunt, he had a new and bold invention to spring upon his clients. He had developed a horse-drawn monorail – apparently his own uninfluenced invention, although his priority is in some quarters contested on the grounds of an apparently abortive experiment in Russia a year previously – although this latter differed significantly from Palmer's invention in its details.

Palmer's system consisted of stout wooden baulks, supported approximately 3ft 6in above ground level on equally stout timber posts placed at intervals of 10ft. On top of the baulks were laid wrought-iron rails, described in the *Mechanics' Magazine* in August 1825 as being '4in wide, convex on the top, 1/4in thick at the edges, and 12in thick at

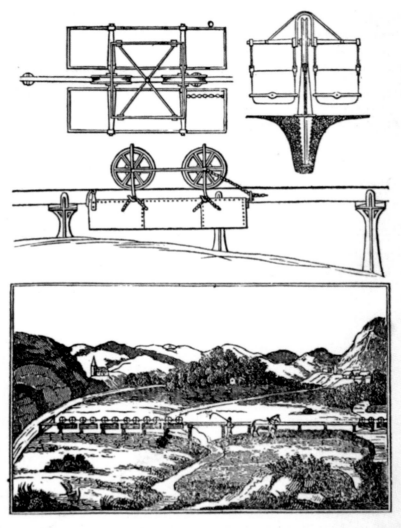

PALMER'S SUSPENSION RAILWAY, 1822, showing carriages with central rail and a general view over irregular country.

(From Elijah Galloway's "History of the Steam Engine.")

Palmer's Deptford monorail.

the centre'. If this account were true, it would make for a very odd section indeed, and being wrought iron rather than cast, the rails would probably have had sufficient inherent strength and resilience to render the timber baulks quite unnecessary. In fact it sounds quite improbable, leading one to suspect that the description is, at least, rather poorly expressed, and in the absence of a clear illustration it is quite hard to envisage precisely what Palmer's rail looked like.

The account in the *Mechanics' Magazine* goes on to describe in fuller detail the construction of this idiosyncratic permanent way, revealing quite a complex assembly, and to judge from the frequency with which 'levelling wedges' are mentioned, rather a difficult one to set up satisfactorily. Coupled with the fact that the entire line was constructed in what was described as a 'dry ditch, nine feet wide', it sounds very much as if Mr Palmer's design obviated most of the now understood benefits of such a system, these being the simple nature of construction and the almost total elimination of the costly groundworks normally associated with rail haulage systems.

When also considering that one horse could pull only two wagons, which implies a capability roughly two-thirds less than that of Whitbread's conventional plateway, one has to wonder whether those who

commissioned Mr Palmer to construct his monorail felt in hindsight that they had really received value for money. Palmer went on to become resident engineer for the London Docks Company, and experimented further with the monorail at Deptford, of which latter installation drawings do exist, indicating a far more sensible use of both land and materials – so presumably (in its inventor's eyes at least) the idea had potential, although it failed to garner the same acceptance as another of his inventions for the LDCo. – galvanized corrugated iron sheeting.

More Monorails

In its defence, the industrial monorail, whilst unusual, is by no means such an outlandish oddity. 'What goes around comes around', as they say, and apart from isolated and peculiar experiments such as the Lartigue system (of which the famous Listowel and Ballybunion Railway in Ireland is perhaps the most notable example), a thoroughly successful, portable modular monorail system was developed by Road Machines (Drayton) Ltd in 1949 and became a successful industrial product – especially for temporary works, where, unlike Mr Palmer's system, its flexibility, impermanence and low cost made it an ideal solution.

The second monorail in Essex – Frederick Hester's curious contraption in 1902.

It is unlikely that monorails will receive any further mention within these pages, being a rather outré mode of transport even in the present day, so it is worth mentioning at this point that Palmer's was not the only monorail constructed in Essex. In 1902, an entrepreneur named Frederick Hester constructed a short monorail (or, as Hester termed it, a 'mono-metal tramway') on Canvey Island for the conveyance of tourists.

This was all part of Hester's grand plan to turn the island into an idyllic holiday resort for smog-choked Londoners eager to escape the capital, which included the development of fashionable villas and a seafront esplanade, as well as a lavish winter gardens and palace. The monorail system was to serve these attractions as well as providing a link to the ferry quay for incoming visitors, and ultimately a link to the GER mainline at Southend.

Although these plans faltered before their full extent could be realized, a part of the monorail was built and operated, although on a far humbler scale than was originally intended. Looking frankly rather homemade, it greatly exceeded Palmer's brainchild in terms of curiosity, and even in terms of economy, the single rail being simply laid on the ground on timber sleepers like a conventional railway line. Above this, the single passenger vehicle balanced precariously on a pair of grooved wheels, prevented from toppling over by two shafts that sprouted from the side of the vehicle, between which was harnessed a rather woebegone horse. The unfortunate animal thus became a stabilizer for the inherently unstable trolley, as well as providing its means of propulsion.

A contemporary publication, *Daly's History of Canvey Island*, hailed the monorail as a unique and innovative form of transport, implying that the concept was Hester's alone; but in fact the Canvey Island system was practically identical to that developed by Henry Jules Caillet in 1896 for use in industrial applications.

Hester had hoped to electrify his monorail and develop it further, but like many of his dreams, it was not to be. He was declared bankrupt in 1906, and his effects were sold at auction – presumably it was at this time that his curious monorail also ceased to operate.

The First Railway Proposals

Whilst the iron tramway certainly showed off the advantages to be gained from rail transport, in this initial stage of development it was of limited practicality as a long-distance transport solution. Longer tram-roads were proposed within East Anglia, most notably from Bishop's Stortford to Clayhithe under the ambitious title of 'Rennie's Northern Rail-Road', and with still greater ambition, one from London to Norwich – but perhaps unsurprisingly, these remained unbuilt, and information relating to them is scarce. The technology of the crude tramway still needed some time to evolve into the railway

Another shot of the Hester monorail.

proper before long-distance routes could be sensibly considered.

But by 1818 things were, both literally and figuratively, starting to move. In the north of England, plans were being tentatively made for what was to become the Stockton and Darlington Railway, finally incorporated by Act of Parliament in 1821 and engineered by the great George Stephenson. This would come to be recognized as the first 'proper' railway, hauling passengers and freight between two major cities, and hauled (for freight initially, at least) by 'locomotive engines'.

The Norfolk & Suffolk Rail-Road

The ripples of this new technological revolution percolated into East Anglia in 1824, when large and florid (in their prose, at least) advertisements appeared in the *Norfolk Chronicle* and other regional papers, inviting subscription to the 'Norfolk & Suffolk Rail-Road Company'. This enterprise sought to drive a rail link through the counties of Norfolk, Suffolk and Essex into London, and described in flamboyant terms the many benefits to trade that would result from such a link, all for the bargain sum of £980,000.

These advertisements turned up late in December of that year, along with a character recorded only as 'Mr Smith', who had arrived in Bury St Edmunds hot foot from London on Christmas Eve. It is difficult not to conjure up images of Dickensian snow-swept streets and tall hats as the stranger failed (perhaps unsurprisingly, since it was Christmas Eve) to seek out a local solicitor by the name of Borton. Presumably Mr Smith spent his Christmas in Bury, because a few days later he succeeded in making contact with Mr Borton, who, he hoped, would be interested in a proposition from one Mr J. Wilkes, in whose name he was apparently acting.

Wilkes was a junior partner in a firm of solicitors, Wilkes & Verbecke of New Broad Street, London – who in their turn were acting on behalf of the promoters of this bold new scheme. Their business with Borton was, on the face of it, simple: they wished him to drum up subscriptions for their share issue in the County of Suffolk, presumably believing that Borton's knowledge and local reputation would remove any potential doubts in the minds of rural investors.

In this last assumption they were rather wide of the mark. Presumably it was due to no blot on Borton's personal escutcheon, but the 'Railway Mania' of the 1830s was still some years away, and his well-meaning approaches were met with a marked lack of enthusiasm from would-be investors, much to the frustration of Wilkes and Verbecke. Smith, the emissary (Wilkes charmingly referred to him in correspondence as his 'factotum'), remained in Bury St Edmunds until New Year's Day, returning to London presumably with the sense of a job well done – but soon after his return difficulties started to appear.

A letter to the *Bury and Norwich Post* was published on 5 January: this questioned the need for a railway that would serve towns that already had good communications via the existing waterways, and it also questioned the propriety of the promoter's approach, particularly their practice of soliciting for the uptake of shares without indulging in the formality of holding public meetings to complement their eulogistic prospectuses. Perhaps the London promoters had not bargained for the caution of East Anglian landowners, but few, if any shares were sold in the region, and no one of any reputation would allow their name to be associated with the promotion.

By 19 January – for whatever their failings, these early promoters did not want for energy – a new prospectus had appeared, naming the company directors and, significantly, the engineer who had been instructed to prepare the plans and sections for the route – one Mr Henry Palmer, presumably now no longer wedded to monorails, and apparently no longer implacably opposed to railways.

The Process of Planning a Railway

A note here would perhaps not go amiss on the legal procedure for implementing a public railway at the time, as it becomes a defining part of the narrative for all proposed railways discussed later. In simple terms, a prospectus was issued to gather shareholders, thus raising the necessary capital to proceed with the initial surveys and the formation of a promoting company. An engineer would be appointed to survey the route, hopefully with an eye both to efficiency of operation and eventual capital cost, preparing an in-depth proposal that would form the basis of an application for an Act of Parliament; this in its turn, if granted, would give the company powers to compulsorily purchase the land needed from the private landowners.

Simple in theory, this proved less practicable in reality, as not all landowners wanted railways ploughing through their property, and during the railway boom of the 1830s and 1840s it was not uncommon for engineers and their assistants to face hostile and even violent opposition from the landowners for what often amounted to a professional trespass upon their land. Subsequent surveys would then have to be submitted to a Clerk of the Peace in every county traversed, prior to the completed proposal being submitted to Parliament. Come the 1840s, when Parliament sought to stem the apparently limitless flow of improbable schemes, a time limit was set on these submissions, resulting in many undignified scenes as rushed proposals were flung on to the desks of the local clerks by panting solicitors, arriving on steaming horses to hammer on the doors mere minutes before the midnight deadline in a desperate bid to deposit their plans.

When, and if, the parliamentary act was granted, power was given to the companies to call upon their shareholders for funds up to a limit set by the act, a limit that developed a tendency to be modified by further acts as costs almost inevitably overran – often to the chagrin of the shareholders. Of this, more anon, as it became an almost universal rite of passage for any major route.

The Plans Start to Unravel

By the time of the shareholders' meeting in March 1826 there were some rather significant problems appearing on the horizon for the Norfolk, Suffolk & Essex Rail-Road, as it had by now become. Only a small proportion of the total shareholding had been taken up, and there was scant enthusiasm for the project amongst the East Anglian landowners. Palmer had submitted his fee invoice, but had thus far received nothing beyond his expenses. Other fees were owing, and those that had been paid stood up poorly to dispassionate scrutiny, casting doubt upon the integrity of some of the directors, and not least upon the mysterious and remote character of Mr Wilkes. The upshot of all this was the appointment of a Committee of Inquiry, which had the double-edged effect of making Mr Wilkes seem altogether rather less mysterious, but also far shadier than the worried shareholders might be supposed to have liked.

Wilkes, it transpired, had his fingers in a number of pies – his involvement, for example, in the Cornwall and Devon Mining Company had somehow lost that company quite a large sum of money (a large proportion of it, one presumes, somehow finding its way into the pockets of Mr Wilkes). He had also contrived to become MP for Sudbury – perhaps wisely from his point of view, as it was at that time impossible for a seated MP to be imprisoned for debt – but those who backed his political campaign had found, as the Rail-Road Company was now finding, that their out-of-pocket expenses on his behalf were proving impossible to recoup. A charge of forgery against him – by the British Annuity Company – collapsed, and he died in 1846 without apparently paying any of his debts, regardless of whether they were financial or societal.

It is difficult, in retrospect, to discern whether the Norfolk, Suffolk and Essex Rail-Road was a swindle from start to finish, or simply a well-intentioned (albeit rather optimistic) scheme that had the misfortune to be hijacked by an opportunist crook, but the end result was still the same. The Norfolk, Suffolk and Essex Rail-Road, which, had it been completed, would have been a bold and notable pioneer alongside the Stockton and Darlington and Liverpool and Manchester Railways, was never built. It would be another ten years before East Anglia joined the railway revolution, but at least Wilkes, and his factotum Smith, had sown a seed of interest that would bear liberal fruit in the years to come.

Other (Less Criminal) Schemes

Oddly enough, whilst all this high-profile chicanery was going on, Henry Palmer, clearly rather less concerned about canal navigation in the east than he had been in the north, was promoting a railway scheme of his own – from London to Ipswich. This enthusiasm on Palmer's part was no doubt connected with the fact that he had been engaged to survey and engineer a new dock for Ipswich, but ultimately his grand plan for the railway, whilst rather more scrupulous than that of his contemporaries on the Norfolk & Suffolk, likewise came to nothing.

Like Palmer, others were gaining a taste for the new railways, and further schemes now started to appear hot on the heels of one another – proposals for the Ipswich and Suffolk Railway were advanced by a Messrs Cubitt and Alexander, following swiftly on from Palmer in 1825. After them, in 1827, came a Mr Walker and his Bury to Ipswich Railway, whilst the boldly titled Grand Northern and Eastern Railway, under the aegis of one Mr Cundy, followed in 1834, accompanied that year by Mr Gibbs and his plans for the Great Northern Railway. These last three are significant, because although only one of them came to fruition (albeit in drastically reduced form), the people involved in its promotion would soon play an important part in the development of the first railway to be built in East Anglia.

CHAPTER 2

The Eastern Counties Railway

Whilst the machinations relating to the Norfolk, Suffolk and Essex Railroad in 1824 and the more honest schemes that followed in its footsteps were unsuccessful, they had at least fostered a growing

The Family Concern: Cobbold, Cobbold & Chevallier

John Cobbold (1774–1877), a prominent brewer in Ipswich, had previously been involved with the unsuccessful Bury St Edmunds–Ipswich route promoted by James Walker. Cobbold and his son, confusingly named John *Chevallier* Cobbold, had been members of a committee established to drive the scheme forwards. Evidently their failure had by no means dampened their spirits, for in 1836 John Cobbold appeared on the roll of directors for the proposed Grand Eastern Counties Railway, along with his brother-in-law, Dr Chevallier (another confusing complication of names) who had also been involved in promoting Walker's scheme. The son, John Chevallier Cobbold, in his turn became the solicitor to the Eastern Counties Railway, making the whole business something of a family affair.

interest in the new technology of the steam-hauled railway. Encouraged by the success of George Stephenson's landmark projects in the north of England – the Stockton and Darlington in 1825, and the Liverpool and Manchester in 1830 – the commercial benefits that resulted from a connection with the new iron roads were coming into focus. East Anglia thus far had witnessed only abortive schemes, but there were those who were determined that the Railway Age should not bypass the east of England for much longer.

The First Forays: 1834

The story of the Eastern Counties Railway, destined to be not only the first railway in East Anglia, but also arguably the most controversial, began in 1834, when two rival railway schemes, both originating outside East Anglia, were promoted. Both were intended to connect the city of York with the capital – one was the Grand Northern and Eastern Railway, surveyed by the canal engineer Nicholas Cundy in 1834, and the other the Great Northern Railway, surveyed by Joseph Gibbs, not to be confused with the later and better-known Great Northern Railway, with which it shares no connection.

Both routes connected York to London via Cambridge, and this promise of a line passing albeit

John Braithwaite.

John Braithwaite (1797–1870)

Braithwaite is now perhaps less well known for his role as a civil engineer than he is for constructing one of the 'also-rans' of the Rainhill locomotive trials undertaken by the Liverpool and Manchester Railway in 1829 (at which the Stephensons' *Rocket* became famous as the clear winner, and infamous for running over and fatally wounding the Right Hon. William Huskisson, MP for Liverpool). Braithwaite's entry, *The Novelty*, owed much of its impressive speed and agility to being far too lightly constructed either to do any useful work or to stand up to heavy usage without disintegrating, as its subsequent failure in the trials rather brutally illustrated. No doubt the provisional directors of the Grand Eastern Counties Railway hoped that Braithwaite was sounder on civil engineering matters than he was on those mechanical.

briefly through East Anglia galvanized local interest in railway speculation. Thus a prospectus was issued for a new railway linking London to Yarmouth via Ipswich and Norwich, surveyed by the engineer John Braithwaite.

Plans and Parliamentary Approval

The route of the new line was to start from the outskirts of London at Shoreditch, then go through Colchester and on to Ipswich, heading thence to Norwich and to Yarmouth via Scole. Application was made via a parliamentary bill in February of 1836, coinciding with the bills for the previously mentioned GNR and the GN&ER, both strongly opposing the application of the Eastern Counties Railway. (The 'Grand' prefix was fairly quickly dropped, something of a portent of things to come.) The ECR cannot have been seen as a direct competitor to either, but it seems likely that both of the northern companies saw extension into East Anglia as being their own just reward for venturing into what was then virgin railway territory.

The ECR bill received parliamentary assent on 4 July in that year, as did that of the GN&ER, the competing bill for the GNR having been defeated at its second reading. Thus the way was laid open for a truly East Anglian railway, a total of 126 miles (203km) long, and at the time the longest railway then sanctioned by Parliament. With an alacrity characteristic of early railway promoters, the construction of the line was scheduled to commence the following year.

Flushed with this success, the family concern of Cobbold, Cobbold & Chevallier was also pushing throughout the latter part of 1836 to revive proposals for an Ipswich–Bury railway similar to Walker's scheme, with which they had previously been associated, but differing from it in making a connection with the proposed ECR at Belstead, near Ipswich. Sadly this independent plan met with no more success than Walker's, and Bury would remain the unattained focus of railway speculation for some years to come.

Despite initial promise, the share take-up for the ECR in East Anglia, rather like that of the abortive

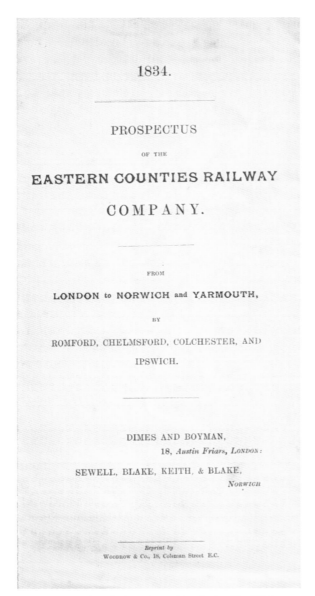

1834.

PROSPECTUS

OF THE

EASTERN COUNTIES RAILWAY

COMPANY.

FROM

LONDON to NORWICH and YARMOUTH,

BY

ROMFORD, CHELMSFORD, COLCHESTER, AND

IPSWICH.

DIMES AND BOYMAN,
18, *Austin Friars*, LONDON:

SEWELL, BLAKE, KEITH, & BLAKE,
NORWICH

Reprint by
Woodrow & Co., 18, Coleman Street E.C.

The beginning of the Railway Age in East Anglia. The 1834 prospectus for the proposed Eastern Counties Railway.

scheme that preceded it, was poor. The bulk of the shareholding was ultimately purchased by investors in the industrial North, already familiar with railways, although the promise of suspiciously high dividends should have rung alarm bells for those in the know, and possibly played a part in discouraging local investment in an area not yet afflicted by the fiscal blindness that was a symptom of 'Railway Mania'. Be it due to prescience or folly, the lack of local shareholding was to cause problems in East Anglia in the years to come.

Furthermore, there were hints that the conduct of the Eastern Counties Company during the bill's passage through Parliament had been less than scrupulous. R.S. Joby, in his book *The Eastern Counties Railway*, compares the whipping up of support for the new line to the Eatanswill election, that parody of political corruption in Charles Dickens' *Pickwick Papers*, then being serialized throughout 1836. (In fact the comment strikes even closer to home, as biographers of Dickens believe that Eatanswill was based on Sudbury, in Suffolk – particularly its election of 1835, upon which Dickens had reported for the *Morning Chronicle*. Sudbury had gained a reputation for being one of the most politically corrupt locations in the country – remember, the shady Mr Wilkes had become its MP in Chapter One – and as a result was disenfranchised in the 1840s.)

Gladstone implied darkly in Parliament that those who had signed a petition supporting the ECR 'got a good lunch' – although in comparison to the later behaviour of the ECR, this bit of light bribery was a fairly mild misdemeanour. The GN&ER's objection to the bill, as a prime example, was speedily and efficiently quashed by the simple expedient of handing over no less than £2,050 to sweeten the pill.

Construction Commences: 1837

Parliamentary consent having been won by fair means or foul, the construction of the new line started early in 1837, work commencing at the London end – although it appears that some surprisingly crucial details had still not been worked out, such as the decision over the gauge to which the new line should be laid. That the now standard gauge of 4ft 8½in was the only sensible choice may appear obvious in hindsight, but was far from being so in 1837. In the west of the country, Brunel's 7ft broad gauge was still in the ascendant, displaying a stability and speed that was unparalleled; and the penalties attending inconsistencies of gauge were a bogeyman as yet only dimly visible on the horizon.

That said, it is still hard to justify the eventual choice of a 5ft gauge, being so nearly-but-not-quite the standard (or Stephenson's) gauge, and quite a long way off Brunel's expansive (and expensive) 7ft gauge with its attendant advantages of comfort and speed. Whilst at least numerically tidy, there were very few railways of 5ft gauge built in the British Isles, and inevitably this short-sighted and rather indefensible decision would come back to bite the directors in due course.

By the winter of 1838 disappointingly little progress had been made, work having taken place over a mere 25 miles (40km) or so of the total route, and barely reaching within the borders of Essex. The shareholders were becoming unsettled, as well they might, the regular calls that were being made upon their shares not appearing to match the level of progress on the ground.

There were a number of reasons behind this. Foremost amongst them was an inexpert assessment by Braithwaite of the costs required to purchase the land and recompense its occupants. The Act of Parliament granted to a new railway gave the promoting company a right to compulsorily purchase the land needed, but did not preclude them from having to pay compensation to the former owners, especially if it could be proved that any loss of income would be incurred by the landowner as a result. The wealthier the occupant, the harder it was to palm them off, the landed gentry having the political, financial and legal might to make life difficult for a putative railway company, especially as financial problems were de rigueur in this new business of building railways.

The poor, conversely, could be conveniently swept away at almost no expense to the railway developers – and all too frequently were, especially in those instances where the railways were creeping into the overpopulated (and therefore cheap) fringes of London.

Furthermore the construction of the early railways was no picnic. Now that we are inured to the wonders of rail travel we take it for granted, but no major route on today's network is without its toll of death and debilitating injury dating back to the years during which it was built. The early railways were built with brute force and manual labour by itinerant bands of navvies, hard-working, hard-drinking men who hacked out cuttings, embankments and tunnels with picks, shovels and wheelbarrows – unless stubborn terrain demanded the use of dangerous and unpredictable explosives, inevitably pushing a routinely high death toll even higher.

The ECR was no exception, and the problems encountered over a mere 25 miles (40km) of line were reflected in the escalating costs. Building a railway out of London was still a new and expensive exercise – like the earlier London & Greenwich Railway, which opened in 1836, the ECR planned to build

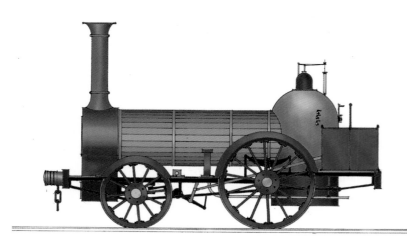

Bury & Co. 2-2-0 locomotive of the Eastern Counties Railway.

their route out of the capital on a series of arches, this being cheaper than purchasing and clearing the ground that would otherwise be necessary, but still expensive. Beyond this viaduct, the route was to run over an embankment built upon the Bow marshes, boggy, treacherous land that absorbed the shareholders' money as surely as it absorbed the spoil that was continually tipped into it. It was not until the line passed Stratford that ground conditions improved – but still the costs continued to mount up.

The plan had been that construction would commence at each end of the line and progress towards a union in the middle; but the problems at the London end soon forced a rethink. The minority of shareholders resident in East Anglia had worked hard to prepare for the coming of the line, using their influence to negotiate terms with local landowners reluctant to accommodate the passage of a railway across their property, and many of the shareholders themselves were land or business owners hopeful for the prosperity that a railway connection to the capital would bring.

The neglect of the Norfolk end of the line thus caused a great deal of frustration amongst the East Anglian contingent, but due to the disproportionate take-up by northern shareholders, who were far more interested in healthy dividends than the well-being of the rural economy, they were increasingly finding themselves voices crying in the wilderness. In August 1838 at the General Meeting the ominous announcement was made that, due to financial constraints, the work beyond Colchester would be 'temporarily' suspended.

Rural Dissidents

Foremost amongst the East Anglian shareholders angered by this decision were of course the Cobbolds and Dr Chevallier. It seemed clear to them that the ECR was about to make a concerted effort to wriggle out of their obligations to East Anglian interests, and the Cobbolds felt that it was their responsibility to ensure that this did not happen. The odds, however, were stacked against them. The ECR board held a rule stipulating that six directors should be nominated for retirement at the General Meeting every year, any retiring member then having the option to stand for re-election at the same meeting. Crucially, this nomination of retirees was decided not by lot, but by ballot, which meant that majority interests could very effectively control the make-up of the board and block troublesome interference; and this, for the Cobbolds and Dr Chevallier, meant a struggle against an inexorably rising tide.

Local influence on the board was progressively whittled away through this means, the vacant places invariably being taken up by men from London or the North, until inevitably John Cobbold senior was nominated for retirement, in 1839. His ally, Dr Chevallier, had already resigned prior to this, having felt that his position on the board was no longer compatible with his calling as a clergyman. This left only the son, J.C. Cobbold, remaining, and to him it must have been evident that the writing was on the wall.

After the retirement of John Cobbold Snr, the Cobbolds made an appeal to the High Court in an attempt to compel the ECR to adhere to the terms of its contract to construct the line in its entirety. The Company, in response, argued that they had to act in the interests of the majority of their shareholders, and the court decided in their favour.

The Cobbolds' next move was a remarkable, if rather optimistic, piece of élan: to attempt the passage of a parliamentary bill that would bind the erring ECR into a sort of 'tit-for-tat' arrangement – once the line had reached Chelmsford, they suggested, no more work would be carried out at that end until the eastern end had been started, and so forth. The proposed bill would further insist that local interests were proportionately represented on the board of directors, and that the share capital of the company should be increased to support these ends.

The final breathtaking stipulation was that the cost of the bill brought by the Cobbolds should be borne not by them, but by the ECR itself – a bold, if perhaps not very diplomatic suggestion. Not surprisingly, the bill was thrown out at its second reading.

For appearances' sake, the ECR maintained their claim that the cessation of operations at Colchester was only a temporary measure; however, the wider

A contemporary depiction of an Eastern Counties train departing from Shoreditch. It appears to be hauled by one of the 2-2-0 locomotives assigned to passenger duties in the early years of the ECR, but rather illustrates just how unfamiliar artists of the time were with the new technology.

opinion of the shareholders and directors suggested that in truth, the line would progress no further. J.C. Cobbold had reported one such shareholder antagonistic to his manoeuvrings, commenting: 'If you want a rail-road in Suffolk, you must make it yourselves.' This may have been a throwaway comment intended to dismiss the troublesome solicitor, but ultimately it proved to be prophetic.

1839: The Opening of the Eastern Counties Railway

When the Eastern Counties Railway (the ECR) finally opened to traffic in 1839, it was a far more modest affair than had originally been intended. Far from being the longest line sanctioned by Parliament, the new line covered a mere 10 miles (16km) only, from Mile End to Brentwood in Essex, although this did not deter the directors from staging a grand opening, a formality that was clearly deemed obligatory for any such opening at the time, no matter how far short of its goal the new line had fallen.

True to form, two heavy trains waited at Mile End station to receive the huge party of directors, dignitaries and illustrious guests – most of whom were no doubt taken aback by the temporary building and the less than salubrious neighbourhood in which it was located. Amongst these dignitaries was the Persian ambassador, who was left behind after his late arrival; a hastily assembled train of two vehicles was sent back to retrieve him and his party.

Such embarrassing setbacks aside, the two trains, their pale blue liveried coaches hauled by elegant

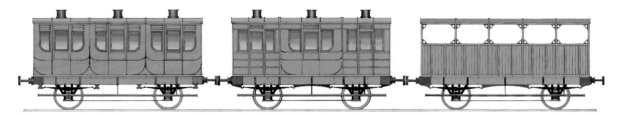

First, composite and open third-class coaches of the ECR.

BISHOPSGATE STATION.

Shoreditch (later Bishopsgate) station, the original terminus of the ECR.

but diminutive 2-2-0 locomotives built in the Bury fashion, were despatched up the line to the sound of cannon fire and the accompaniment of the band of the Coldstream Guards, to view the as yet uncompleted works at Shoreditch. Here the party was given a tour of the partly completed terminus, a large and imposing Italianate building that sat uncomfortably with the temporary wooden stations found elsewhere on the ECR at that time.

Once they had absorbed all there was to be absorbed, they then clambered aboard the train back to Romford, where an extensive buffet luncheon had been laid on. Naturally this luncheon was followed in the evening by an even more sumptuous dinner, at which extensive speeches, toasts and heavily ladled compliments were given for the benefit of those who had brought this, East Anglia's premier railway, to fruition. The *Railway Magazine*, in its account of proceedings, felt it necessary to point out that no accidents were recorded on the day. This didn't last, as the derailment of a locomotive in the following month killed both driver and fireman. The accident was attributed to excessive speed, something that ECR passengers only a few years later would have found difficult to credit indeed.

By 1840, the ECR had still only managed to extend to Shoreditch, the grand terminus having now been completed (although in a neighbourhood hardly more

The old Railway Station (By-gone Colchester)

An unusual postcard view of the old ECR temporary railway station at Colchester.

Peto's ill-fated hotel constructed opposite the ECR station at Colchester. This building was later given to the town by Peto for use as an asylum.

alluring than that of Mile End), and to Colchester by 1843, where another cheap, temporary wooden station was constructed.

As if to rub salt into the wound, a Grand Hotel was built to serve the station by the contractor and speculator Samuel Morton Peto, who himself played a large part in the later development of railways in the region, and had in fact tendered (unsuccessfully) for the Shoreditch contract. Another impressive Italianate pile, the hotel was unsuccessful as a venture, leading Peto to hand it over for use as an insane asylum in 1849. Whether or not the optimism for greater prosperity thanks to the railway was misplaced is a moot point, but certainly it was at Colchester in 1843 that progress on the line, and apparently the ambitions of the ECR, finally expired.

A Change in Approach

If anyone had ever entertained the slender hope that the ECR board might, when the financial situation improved, turn their minds once again to the completion of the line into Norfolk, then those hopes were soon to be dashed. Far from focusing on their obligations in Norfolk, the ECR began to explore the easier profits to be made by expanding outwards from their Colchester territory. The first indication of this new approach was the promotion of a new branch from Colchester to Harwich, a move that justly infuriated business interests in Ipswich, as the town had poured a great deal of money into the redevelopment of the docks there in anticipation of the extra traffic that the coming of the railway would generate.

Now it became clear that not only would the promised railway not be coming, but if the projection of a branch to Harwich were successful, the huge increase in shipping traffic that Ipswich had been hoping for would now become a windfall for the docks at Harwich, and the investment made at Ipswich would go to waste for the want of a railway connection. As it happened, Harwich did not gain a railway connection until 1854, but the treachery on the part of the ECR was not forgotten in Ipswich, and indeed did much to pave the way for the creation of the Eastern Union Railway in 1846, which is the subject of the next chapter.

Samuel Morton Peto (1809–1889)

Peto's name nowadays does not command the same level of recognition as some of his contemporaries, but in the mid 1840s he is reputed to have been one of the largest employers of labour in the world. His name is perhaps best known in East Anglia, where he played a significant part in developing the railway infrastructure of the region, although he was not a local man, having been born in Surrey in 1809.

Starting his career as a bricklayer with a family firm, by 1830 Peto had entered into partnership with Thomas Grissell, a union that proved successful, because over the subsequent seventeen years they carried out a number of large projects in London, including work on Bazalgette's great sewer system and the new Houses of Parliament, as well as the erection of Nelson's Column and the Lyceum Theatre.

Grissell & Peto became involved with the Northern & Eastern Railway's extension to Hertford, and had been sole engineers for the first railway in Norfolk, the Yarmouth & Norwich Railway, thanks to the agency of that line's engineer, Robert Stephenson. Grissell eventually dissolved the partnership in 1846, feeling that Peto's methods of running a business involved too many risks, but by 1848 Peto had found a new business partner in the form of his brother-in-law Edward Betts.

Sir Samuel Morton Peto. A prolific contractor in the 1840s, Peto made a significant impact on the commercial landscape of East Anglia, both as a contractor to the railways and as a developer in his own right.

They must have inspired confidence, as they later formed a triumvirate with the established contractor Thomas Brassey as Peto, Brassey & Betts. By this point, Peto was at the centre of an international business building railways; he was made a baronet in recognition of his work building railways in the Crimea during the conflict.

He received further honours from Denmark for the construction of railway links that enabled a thriving trade with Britain via the port of Lowestoft on the east coast – a town that has more reason than most to remember Peto. Naturally he was responsible for the town's rail link, but he also invested heavily in the redevelopment of the town as a successful holiday location, as well as a focus for import, export and industry.

Peto's fingerprints are all over the railway network in East Anglia, and he is immortalized not only by a bust at Norwich station, but in Peto Way in Lowestoft, a road that branches off Denmark Road (itself a nod to Peto's Danish connection), Peto Avenue (and Peto Road) in Colchester, and Morton Peto Road in Yarmouth.

Next on the list of infidelities was the promotion in 1843 of the Eastern Counties, Stratford and Thames Junction Railway – intended, as its name suggests, to provide a link between the ECR at Stratford and the Thames at North Woolwich. Opening in 1846 with coal traffic being a primary target, it was in theory an independent company but heavily reliant on support from the ECR, into which it was swiftly absorbed in 1847. An extension to Cambridge and Brandon followed in 1845, designed to connect with the Norfolk Railway and thus provide a link (albeit a circuitous one) to Norwich via that company's metals, the contract for the construction of which was awarded to the firm of Grissell & Peto.

Absorption of the Northern & Eastern Railway

A lease of the neighbouring Northern and Eastern Railway (the 'Great' prefix had by now been dropped) had been undertaken by the ECR in 1844, giving access via the extension constructed by Peto to Hockerill and Hertford along the route of the River Lea. The N&ER already enjoyed a connection with the ECR at Stratford, at which point they had built for themselves a depot complete with an elegant locomotive roundhouse to the design of the N&ER's engineer, Robert Stephenson, and similar to that extant at Derby and the remains recently uncovered at Curzon Street, Birmingham, during works relating to HS2.

The N&ER was the rather truncated fulfilment of the plans of the Grand Northern & Eastern Railway, whose ambitions to build a railway from London to York had helped inspire the ECR proposals in the first place. Now much more condensed in its scope, the N&ER was struggling, and dependent on the ECR for access to London, since funds had been insufficient to provide for a London terminus. Because of this, the ECR had, in 1840, compelled the smaller line to adopt the 5ft gauge, although once the lease was completed, the N&ER was further compelled to *re*-lay to 4ft 8½in gauge – this was because by then, the ECR themselves had capitulated in the face of pressure from the standard-gauge Eastern Union Railway.

1845: Enter George Hudson

This growing habit of absorbing other railways into the ECR coincides with the arrival on the board of a new chairman, George Hudson, who replaced Henry Bosanquet, the outgoing chair, in 1845.

Hudson was already a big name by the time he took over the directorship of the ECR in 1845, having secured control over the growing network of railways in and around his home town of York. He had little or no interest in railway traffic in East Anglia, but his policy had always been one of assimilation, and the Eastern Counties, by virtue of their route through Cambridge, held the key to a great ambition: a railway from London to York.

Stratford Works, Eastern Counties Railway. Originally built by the Northern & Eastern Railway, the works were taken over by the ECR when the N&ER was absorbed, and became the focus of locomotive operations thereafter.

George Hudson (1800–1871)

Hudson is one of those characters who are a gift to an author. He was born in Howsham in Yorkshire, in 1800 – which was quite appropriate, because despite the dubious reputation he acquired in later years, he played an important part in shaping the century he lived in. Born into a prosperous farming family, he distinguished himself early on by fathering an illegitimate child at the age of fifteen and being driven out of the village.

This disgrace became the catalyst for his remarkable career, as he gravitated to York, securing a job at a draper's shop, where he rose quickly to a partnership in the business and married one of the draper's daughters – two facts possibly not entirely unconnected. He also showed a surprising solicitude towards an elderly uncle of his who lived in York, which bore fruit when the uncle, a wealthy property owner, left the ambitious young man his entire estate, which in modern terms would have made George a millionaire overnight.

If an air of doubtful morality hung around these early fortunes, it was characteristic of things to come. George invested his legacy in the up-and-coming business opportunity of the railways, where many had lost huge sums – but Hudson was no fool, and through blustering arrogance, a lavish hospitality budget and some financial legerdemain, made huge sums before his somewhat tragic fall from grace.

An up-by-the-bootstraps Yorkshireman, George Hudson came to represent the Railway Mania as the self-styled 'Railway King'. Revered and despised in equal measure, his successes were only matched in dramatic effect by his swift downfall.

His *modus operandi* here was typical of his policy for most of his smoothly acquired directorships, and the ECR exhibited all the qualities required. It was an existing line with a route he needed; it was floundering in the mire; it had an army of unhappy shareholders baying for its blood. These factors played into the hands of the visionary Hudson.

The first step was to invite himself to a shareholders' meeting of the company concerned. His appearance would generally strike fear into the hearts of the directors, and a spark of hope in those of the shareholders. He would confidently promise a sharp increase of dividends, up to 9 or 10 per cent – assuming that by some chance he were elected chairman of the board, a motion that was usually quickly passed – and in short order the company, hitherto in dire straits, would somehow find itself forging profitable links with its neighbours, reducing operating costs, and, lo and behold, meagre (or sometimes non-existent) dividends would suddenly leap up to the promised 10 per cent. The shareholders would be ecstatic, their decision would be apparently

How the other half lives: first-class accommodation on the ECR in 1847.

A FIRST-CLASS CARRIAGE (EASTERN COUNTIES RAILWAY) IN 1847.

vindicated, and Hudson would be their revered hero and the master of all he surveyed. Those who had fallen before the Hudsonian juggernaut, or felt somehow that some devilry was afoot, had not a leg to stand on.

It worked well as a technique. Even better, as Hudson knew full well, whilst the dividends were good, no one worried too much about checking the balance sheet or asking questions, and this was perhaps most crucial to Hudson's plans.

In truth, the numbers just didn't stack up. The 10 per cent so beloved of the shareholders was being paid directly out of capital, a practice at best unsustainable and at worst highly improper. Crucially, it wasn't actually *illegal* – the large-scale economics of the railways were without precedent, and the legal framework to regulate them was still developing. Furthermore, no matter how welcome the cost-cutting measures were, the worst place to implement them was on a line that had been struggling for many years.

The considerably more frugal second-class accommodation. Third must surely have been unpleasant.

INTERIOR OF A SECOND-CLASS CARRIAGE (EASTERN COUNTIES RAILWAY) IN 1847.

THE
EASTERN COUNTIES RAILWAY COMPANY

OFFERS THE FOLLOWING ADVANTAGES TO

NERVOUS PERSONS.

Trains at REDUCED SPEED to meet their views.

The Rate of Speed is not at all FRIGHTFUL.

For example,—**Hertford** is 21 miles from LONDON by the road,—the time allowed for the second **business** train is **One Hour and Thirty-five Minutes!** *(but the journey is not always accomplished in that time.)* Again,—**Waltham** to LONDON was formerly done in **Thirty-seven Minutes,** the time now allowed is **Fifty-Eight Minutes.**

One of the Officials stated that **"The time allowed was so great that they did not know how to kill it!"**

MR. PUNCH says, "The only **Fast** trains on this Line are those that are **Stuck Fast.**" These afford plenty of time for quiet reflection.

N.B.—A person offers for a Wager to run his Donkey against the Train for one stage, and have time for his Breakfast in the bargain !!!

The Season Tickets may be 10 or 20 per cent. higher than on other Lines, but as the time allowed for seeing the country is so liberal on the part of the Company, the Passengers must not complain. Railway Companies cannot afford to waste **Time** and **Steam** without being paid for it.

(By Authority)

PASSENGERS.

An exercise in satire. A poster poking fun at the infamous ECR. Note the reference to Punch magazine — the appalling nature of the Eastern Counties Railway was a favourite topic for derision within its pages.

Another dig at the ECR. The letter in question was the offer to wager the performance of an old donkey against an express train of the ECR, with odds heavily favouring the donkey.

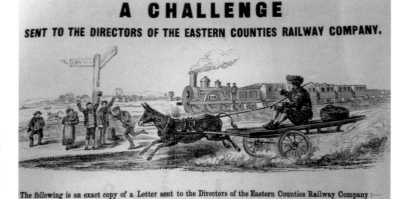

The following is an exact copy of a Letter sent to the Directors of the Eastern Counties Railway Company :—

A backlog of maintenance for locomotives, rolling stock and permanent way required huge injections of cash, not a tightening of the purse strings, so sooner or later the chickens were bound to come home to roost. In addition, many skilled staff were laid off, being replaced by unskilled (and therefore cheaper) labour, creating a situation that was ripe for calamity.

Unsurprisingly, calamity came. An accident on the ECR at Romford in 1846, only a year into Hudson's tenure, was attributed by the Board of Trade to the parlous state of the stock and track and the unskilled nature of the staff, all thanks to Hudson's swingeing economies. Naturally this type of scrutiny made the shareholders a little uncomfortable, although not perhaps as uncomfortable as they would become a few short years later in 1878, when their precious dividends were showing unmistakable signs of shrinking.

All of that, however, lay securely out of sight in 1845, when George Hudson reigned supreme as the Railway King, a pejorative title bestowed by the Rev. Sydney Smith – a popular satirist of the time whose barbs seem rather at odds with his calling – but which was adopted gleefully by Hudson, a known self-publicist. Nor would the directors of the ECR

have been minded to disagree – or at least, not in the initial years of Hudson's tenure. The Romford accident aside, there was a definite upturn in the fortunes of the ECR following Hudson's appointment, as passenger receipts at the Shoreditch terminus rose with a growth in traffic, and a period of further expansion took place in line with his ambition to complete a route to the north of England.

Hudsonian Expansion

A union with the North Midland Railway, already firmly ensconced in the Hudson portfolio, was the key to this plan, and the extension of the ECR to Peterborough via March and Ely was designed to contribute to this goal. The increase in traffic that this generated also led to the expansion of the Shoreditch terminus in 1847, concurrent with the development of the old N&ER works at Stratford into a new depot; this created an extensive complex that would remain at the heart of the Eastern railway network for well over one hundred years. Property was also developed in the locality for railway employees in what became known as 'Hudson Town'.

Further expansion in Cambridgeshire took in the towns of Wisbech and St Ives, whilst an arrangement

Share certificate of the Ely & Huntingdon Railway. Typical of share certificates of the era, these florid and confident tokens of investment frequently failed to fulfil their promise, yielding a fraction of their stated value when sold, or purchased as part of the process of amalgamation into another company, as signified by the GER stamp on this example.

with the East Anglian Railway (the EAR) gave the ECR a link to Huntingdon. The EAR was a short-lived concern, formed in 1847 by the amalgamation of the Lynn & Ely Railway, the Lynn & Dereham Railway and the Ely & Huntingdon Railway, all of which opened in 1846.

Perpetually troubled, the EAR had been in negotiations with the ECR regarding a possible lease in 1850, as a result of the Norfolk company having gone into receivership. The resultant offer being less than generous, the EAR turned to the Great Northern for more favourable terms, and an agreement was struck in 1851. However, the Eastern Counties' hat was still in the ring, for whilst the GNR had running powers over the Wisbech–Peterborough section of the ECR, it did not enjoy the same privilege over the short distance between Wisbech and the start of the EAR – a matter of only half a mile. This the ECR refused to grant, installing a barricade across the tracks to drive the point home.

The GNR soon tired of their troublesome acquisition and hastily terminated their lease, leaving the beleaguered little company no choice but to agree terms with the ECR, although the dire unprofitability of this particular line led to friction between the EAR and the ECR, not helped by the aggressive tactics that

Hudson brought with him to the ECR board. Further into East Anglia, the takeover of the Norfolk Railway in 1848 gave a strong foothold in that county, accessing Fakenham and Yarmouth as well as Lowestoft in Suffolk over NR metals. This company had been formed in 1845 by the amalgamation of the Yarmouth & Norwich Railway, the Norwich & Brandon Railway and the little Lowestoft Railway & Harbour Company, and was another enterprise borne out of the ECR's failure to complete their obligations in 1839. Under the ECR, the NR undertook a further extension of their line as far as Dereham.

From London, further branches to Enfield and Maldon, as well as Tilbury in Essex (via an uneasy relationship with the independent London, Tilbury & Southend Railway), were completed in 1849. A further short extension from Edmonton to Enfield opened in the same year, as did the London & Blackwall Extension Railway, a line that promised to join the ECR with the London & Blackwall Railway, which ran from Fenchurch Street to Blackwall, and had opened to traffic in 1840. Despite being a joint effort between the two companies, relations between the L&BR and the ECR were decidedly uneasy, and in fact the extension stopped short of a physical connection with the ECR until 1850, relying up to that point

Hudson was equally lauded and ridiculed in the public press throughout his career, and the celebration of the anti-Hudson factions was fervent when his empire began to fall.

CELEBRATED COMIC SCENE BETWEEN THE RAILWAY CLOWN (Hudson) AND THE INDIGNANT SHAREHOLDERS.

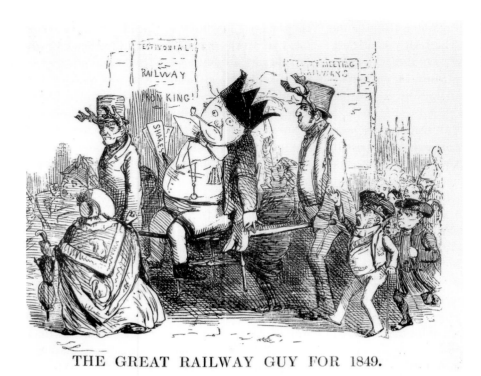

The satirical magazines of the time made great sport at the fall of George Hudson.

THE GREAT RAILWAY GUY FOR 1849.

on a decidedly unsuccessful interchange station at Victoria Park & Bow.

1849: Economic Depression and The Fall of the Railway King

One would have thought that the happiness of the shareholders at all this expansion would have been unalloyed, but forces were at work to dampen their pleasure, especially amongst those with a conscience. Surprisingly, the clouds on the horizon were not entirely of George Hudson's making, although it is certain that his creative approach to accountancy did not help.

The years 1847–1849 were dogged by financial depression, and the fragile bubble of Railway Mania had lost much of its iridescent appeal. Whilst Hudson was by no means the only proponent of the mania, he was arguably its most prominent figure, both loved and loathed in more or less equal measure. If the shareholders were becoming uncomfortable, Hudson himself was squirming. He had for years

ridden the bow-wave of railway mania, growing rich on the profits, legitimate or otherwise, of this huge financial bubble. But bubbles burst, and for Hudson, treading a financial tightrope as he was, this was fatal.

The Eastern Counties, urged on by a Quaker named John Cash, set up a committee of enquiry into Hudson's accounting practices. This turned out to be the breach that started the flood, because led by this example, committees of enquiry now started to spring up wherever George Hudson had once sown his generous dividends.

In April 1849 Hudson was called to give evidence before the ECR board, and his defence was not well received. He resigned his position as chairman, but that did not satisfy the ECR, who were looking for large sums in settlement for their grievances.

It is probably prudent to reflect on Hudson's policies from our safer position some 170 years later. It is true that many of his methods would today be illegal, but were not in fact so at the time. Of greater import is the fact that the shareholders of the ECR, many of them financially minded business men, were glad to receive a magical 10 per cent dividend, and troubled themselves not where it came from. Many must have realized that all was not perhaps quite as it should be, but while the profits were flowing into their pockets they minded not how they came, nor how great a proportion flowed into the pockets of the Railway King. Only when the profits dried up did they start looking for a scapegoat, and Hudson made the ideal target. In fact, the crash was inevitable, though any shareholder who had Hudson as his chairman would have enjoyed a longer summer than those who did not.

However, the true legacy of George Hudson, whatever our opinion of his business ethics, is the vision that he entertained and went so far to realize. What marked Hudson apart from his contemporaries was his ability to see the country's railways as a *network*, rather than a disparate collection of independent lines. He alone is responsible for about half the present-day railway network, having realized that both power and economy lay in consolidation of the railroads; thus he paved the way for the progressive assimilation of lines into bigger and bigger companies. These will be explored further later on in the book.

Later Extensions 1850–1862

Whether Hudson's disappearance from the Board of the ECR had anything to do with, for example, the improvement in relations with the L&BR, is hard to say, but given his tactics it seems likely. Certainly, despite the great man's fall from grace and the financial problems that attended it, exacerbated by recession, the Eastern Counties still continued to develop in the final decade of its existence. In 1851, a branch to Shepreth in Cambridgeshire was opened to traffic, whilst a lease of the Royston & Hitchin Railway, which had opened in 1850, gave access to Hitchin in Hertfordshire, although this was to be short-lived, because after the expiration of the lease the spoils went to the Great Northern Railway.

1854 saw the incorporation of the Newmarket Railway, which had opened to traffic in 1846 with parliamentary approval for three extensions, to Bury St Edmunds, Thetford and Ely. By 1850 the company had gone bankrupt, and as the ECR rather fancied an extension from Thetford to Newmarket, it took over the operation of the line, incorporating the company four years later.

1859 saw the opening of the East Suffolk Railway, another amalgamation created out of the Halesworth, Beccles & Haddiscoe Railway (1854), the Yarmouth & Haddiscoe Railway (1856) and the Lowestoft & Beccles Railway (1858). This gave a convenient route to both Lowestoft and Yarmouth for the ECR. Morton Peto, with his business interests in both towns, was naturally a supporter of these developments, and in fact had attempted to lease both the Y&HR and the L&BR as part of a covert plan to challenge the ECR's dominance over traffic to London, using his influence on the London, Tilbury & Southend Railway to gain access to Fenchurch Street – a plan that perhaps fortunately did not come to pass. The independence of the new ESR was extraordinarily short-lived – the ECR took over the operation of the line's services on the day that it opened, while a connection with Ipswich opened on the same day, linking with the ESR at Woodbridge.

1854: Operation of the EUR

Probably the most significant coup for the ECR in the 1850s came about due to the progressively worsening situation of its old adversary, the Eastern Union Railway, which had been pursuing a similar policy of expansion to that of the ECR, and by so doing had run into financial difficulties. In 1854 an Act of Parliament was issued that allowed the struggling EUR to hand over its operation wholesale to the ECR, in what must have been for some a rather disappointing end to a noble enterprise. The EUR remained, however, a nominally independent company with its own financial identity and property, a situation that would not change until 1862, when the identities of both of the pioneering East Anglian companies would be subsumed into a new and much larger entity: the Great Eastern Railway.

CHAPTER 3

The Eastern Union Railway

The abandonment, be it implied or stated, by the Eastern Counties Railway of their ambitions to build a railway beyond Colchester undoubtedly caused much grief in East Anglia. Not only were the shareholders to be deprived of the railway they had hoped for, but the counties of Norfolk and Suffolk, having been persuaded of the commercial opportunities the railway would bring them, had now seen the rug pulled determinedly from under their collective feet. As we have seen, Ipswich had been redeveloping their docks in anticipation of a rail link, and now it appeared that all that effort and investment would go to waste. Even more disturbing to all parties concerned was the intimation that the ECR were beginning to look elsewhere for their returns, 'playing the field' as it were, and this infidelity only served to deepen the anger of the Suffolk and Norfolk factions.

Enter (Again) the Cobbolds

It seems likely that J.C. Cobbold, still smarting from his unsuccessful attempts to pressure the ECR into completing their route into Norfolk, would have kept himself well informed as far as public opinion on local railways was concerned, and these matters would not have escaped him. Furthermore, his own efforts to call the ECR to order were well known, and thus it is not surprising that he should be at

the centre of any new attempt to fill the breach – to 'build it themselves' in fact, just as the nettled board member had suggested. What is slightly more

John Chevallier Cobbold.

Peter Bruff, engineer for the Eastern Union Railway.

surprising is that the impetus should come, not from Cobbold himself, but from an engineer named Peter Bruff.

Bruff had been employed in the construction of the ECR under Braithwaite, but had been dismissed by him in 1842 – amongst a certain amount of satisfied gloating from the board – over work on the Stanway embankment, for which he was responsible. The official justification for his dismissal was that the work was inferior, a claim agreed on by the directors who inspected it – although to what extent these august gentlemen were in a position to judge is not clear. It is unlikely that Bruff lacked skill as an engineer – his subsequent career argues strongly against the suggestion – but it seems probable that he relied too heavily on his foreman to oversee the works, and did not give them the supervision they required, possibly because he appears to have had his mind on higher things.

As an engineer for the Eastern Counties, Bruff was well aware of the wranglings between the two divided factions within the board regarding the lack of progress beyond Colchester, and clearly saw which way the wind was blowing, and how it might be of benefit to him. Whilst still engaged by the ECR, he started to plan his own route for a railway that would complete the passage to Yarmouth from Colchester, and his plan differed considerably from that originally proposed by Braithwaite.

Braithwaite's route, had it been built in its entirety, would have been expensive. He was a railway engineer of the old school, who believed (justifiably, given the limited performance of the early locomotives) that a line should be as direct and level as possible, which meant going over, under or through any natural obstacles. Bridges and tunnels cost money, and cuttings and embankments, whilst cheaper, still added greatly to the overall expenditure. Bruff sought to avoid such expense wherever possible, planning a gently graded route that kept earthworks and civil engineering works to a practical minimum. Doubtless if he had been imprudent enough to mention this alternative scheme to Braithwaite, it would have caused some tension between them – and would certainly not have helped matters when it came to his dismissal for purported incompetency.

The Birth of the Eastern Union Railway

Bruff was not a man to be put off by such a setback, and his growing ambition may well have been fuelled by his circumstances – reports suggest that he fathered twelve children, and although not all of them survived, it is clear that Mr and Mrs Bruff had charge of a large and expensive family. Still, no matter – Bruff had a railway to build, and even better, he knew exactly who to offer it to. Knowing of the efforts that J.C. Cobbold had made whilst on the ECR board, Bruff took his plans and sections to him to enlist his support – and that of the disillusioned shareholders and entrepreneurs of East Anglia.

If the ECR had failed to engage the interest of Norfolk and Suffolk, then the projected Eastern Union

Railway became its polar opposite. Shareholding in the EUR was enthusiastically taken up in the region, and Ipswich quickly emerged as a town with a controlling interest in the new railway; doubtless this was due in no small part to the dock development so dramatically undermined by the failure of the ECR to extend beyond Colchester, and the fear that if action were not taken, Harwich would succeed where Ipswich now looked set to fail.

Bruff's line was designed to join the ECR at Colchester, but then to deviate from the intended route of the ECR some two miles after, heading through the Stour Valley to Ipswich, where it would burrow through Stoke Hill before carrying on to Scole via Stowmarket, subsequently resuming the original proposed alignment of the ECR and continuing on to Norwich. A branch was to be included from Stowmarket to Bury St Edmunds.

Bruff unveiled this grand plan to the general public at a meeting in Ipswich in 1843, at which it met with considerable approval. A committee was appointed, and it should come as no surprise that both the Cobbolds, father and son, took positions on it. The family concern, it would appear, was back in business.

It is interesting to reflect that the ECR were invited to hold a position on the new committee, a gesture surprisingly magnanimous under the circumstances, although undeniably pragmatic. Notwithstanding, the offer was declined, on the basis that the ECR was planning two new branches, one to Bury St Edmunds and Thetford, and one to Ipswich! This was proof, if any were needed, that the ECR had abandoned any intention of completing the grand route that originally gained them their Act of Parliament. Bury, in particular, must have spent many years wondering which, if any, of the many projected schemes to link their town by rail would come to fruition.

A bill for the construction of the EUR as far as Ipswich was submitted to Parliament on 18 March 1844, with a projected share capital of £200,000. The reason that only the line to Ipswich was sought was to accommodate the proposed extension of the ECR from Brandon to Ipswich (and presumably to counter objections to it). The general response to the bill was positive, as well it might be, considering that the

promotion existed to complete the work left undone by the ECR, which latter had already achieved parliamentary approval.

There were of course objections, not least on the part of the ECR, despite the lengths to which the EUR had gone to accommodate their interests. The basis of the objection was the projected branch to Bury and Thetford, but since this line had not yet been submitted to Parliament, the objection was overruled. The bill for the Eastern Union Railway received its inevitable approval on 19 July 1844.

1844: Construction Commences

With a promptness equal to that of its predecessor, the board for the new EUR was formed with none other than John Chevallier Cobbold as its director; furthermore subsequent events proceeded at such a pace that work could begin in August 1844, under the direction of that famous contractor of the early railways, Thomas Brassey. Brassey was already developing an international career as a railway contractor, being responsible for many early railways in Europe, as well as Great Britain. At the time of his death in 1870, he was estimated to have been responsible for one in every twenty miles of railway constructed *in the world*. He also had a reputation for being a fair and even-handed employer, by no means typical of the contractors of the time, who all too often gave little thought to the wellbeing of the navvies working under them.

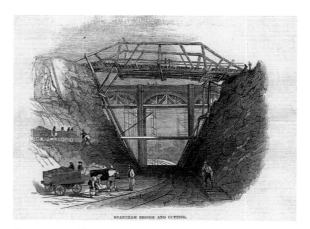

Construction of Brantham bridge and cutting, Eastern Union Railway.

In sharp contrast to the ECR, work on the Eastern Union Railway proceeded quickly, not only being carried out simultaneously at several points along the route, but also at night and on Sundays. The latter issue caused consternation amongst delicate Victorian sensibilities, and was only slightly mitigated by Brassey's insistence that any navvy who wished for a bible would be given one. Nonetheless, progress was sustained under his competent direction, and the full 17 miles (27km) of the EUR was completed to Ipswich by May 1846, something that many in East Anglia must have doubted they would ever see.

The only major hiccup in proceedings had been, perhaps inevitably, at the end-on connection with the ECR at Colchester. Land for the last 2 miles (3km) outside Colchester had already been purchased by the ECR prior to the submission of the EUR bill, although no work had taken place upon it. Thus it was incumbent upon the ECR to complete this section themselves – but as the union of the two railways drew closer, it became apparent that they had not followed the original plans and sections, but had in fact built it with different gradients to favour the intended branch line to Harwich, which had caused so much consternation in Ipswich – although the proposed branch had in fact failed to receive parliamentary assent. The EUR eventually undertook to reconstruct this section, payment for it being due from the ECR at completion.

The connection of these two railways posed another problem for the recalcitrant directors of the ECR. It will be remembered that the ECR was built to the unusual gauge of 5ft, whilst its upstart neighbour, shunning such individualism, had plumped for the standard, or Stephenson's gauge, of 4ft 8½in. In truth, the ECR did not have a leg to stand on. With the exception of the GWR's broad gauge, all of the major routes springing up in Great Britain were being built to the 4ft 8½in gauge, which spread out from the coalfields of the industrial North as the railways matured and found their feet.

Thus, in short order, the financially strapped ECR found themselves saddled with another responsibility, and one for which they had no one but themselves to blame. The entire line, plus the locomotives and rolling stock, would have to be re-gauged to 4ft 8½in – a huge expenditure, and all for the sake of a mere 3½in. It is unlikely that they were pleased, and the new physical union between the ECR and the EUR meant that the relationship between the two railways was now firmly cemented – though it was not always to be a happy one.

Opening of the Eastern Union Railway

The Eastern Union had achieved what the ECR had failed to do: they had built a line that now connected Ipswich to London, and were justified in feeling quite proud of it, even at a time when pride was a defining feature of any new railway, albeit all too frequently followed by a fall.

The formal opening of the Eastern Union Railway took place on 11 June 1846. Freight services had already started over the line, the idea being that the passage of heavy freight trains would do much to consolidate the newly constructed permanent way; this strategy was also in the hope that any teething problems could be ironed out prior to the commencement of passenger traffic, goods being generally easier to placate than human passengers in the event of a problem.

A total of twenty-six locomotives had been ordered by the EUR in 1846, six of them 0-4-2 tender locomotives for goods traffic built by Stothert, Slaughter & Co of Bristol, an early locomotive manufacturer that in 1864 became the Avonside Engine Co. – after this

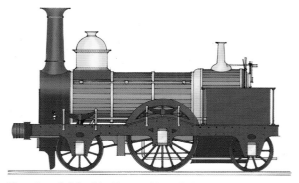

Sharp Bros 2-2-2 of the Eastern Union Railway.

they concentrated increasingly on the manufacture of standard industrial types. The remaining twenty locomotives were 2-2-2 tender locomotives built for passenger service, three of them, Nos 11–13, built by R. & W. Hawthorn of Newcastle, the remainder all being built by Sharp Brothers of Manchester.

All of these bore local names as well as their running numbers, although not all names are recorded: *Suffolk* (No. 9), *Essex* (No. 10) and *Stour* (No. 6) are some of the names that remain to give us a flavour, whilst Nos 1 and 2 appropriately carried the names *Colchester* and *Ipswich* respectively: these two, resplendent in their fresh green livery, would have greeted the invited guests who set foot upon Ipswich platform in anticipation of their first journey over a truly East Anglian railway. On the footplate of the leading engine was no less a personage than Peter Bruff, nominally 'in charge' of the inaugural train – and quite properly, since the entire event was due in no small part to his own initiative back in 1842.

The train was composed of a mixture of open and closed carriages, and was loaded to the gunwales with persons of influence – directors, shareholders, local worthies and invited guests; it left Ipswich at 10:30 after a short ceremony to travel to Colchester. En route many local people had gathered at the lineside to cheer the train through, and the arrival at Colchester was efficient and prompt, the train pulling into the ECR station at 11:45; this was in good time to meet the train from London carrying further worthies, officials and invitees of the ECR to add to the guest list of the forthcoming celebrations.

Amongst them was the director of the ECR, George Hudson himself, who was never a man to miss out on a banquet – especially a banquet that could have interesting repercussions *vis à vis* his business interests. Many a fledgling railway had pause for thought when Hudson turned up at the opening ceremony.

Once the usual formalities had been concluded, the vehicles of the ECR train were then coupled to the Eastern Union train, and the whole lengthy consist was then hauled *back* to Ipswich, arriving at 1:30pm in time for a sumptuous luncheon.

Nor was that the end of it all. When Victorian England celebrated the opening of a railway, they did it in some style – and after an afternoon of diverse amusements, the party gathered once more for an even more sumptuous dinner at the Assembly Rooms in Ipswich, this being in fact the formal celebratory repast.

Typically, the feast to which the directors and shareholders sat down was paralleled in its richness by the feast of flattery and eulogism that characterized the lengthy speeches. Not least amongst them was John Cobbold proposing the good health of George Hudson – itself a doubtful premise, since

The first ECR station at Ipswich, known as Ipswich Stoke Hill.

Hudson was badly afflicted by gout – and the hope that the differences between the EUR and the ECR might now be forgotten. Hudson, in his turn, assured Cobbold and the assembled company that he would bend himself to promoting the joint interests of both companies – no doubt said with his fingers firmly crossed, as many of those before him would already have realized that George Hudson's word in business matters was unreliable indeed.

Problems – and the Ipswich & Bury Railway

One of the problems facing the EUR was that it was far more dependent on the rather thuggish ECR – since 1845 under the chairmanship of George Hudson, who could muster a fine line in thuggishness himself, if occasion demanded – than the ECR was on the EUR. The line from Ipswich relied heavily on the connection to London via ECR metals from Colchester onwards, so the Eastern Union could to some extent hold the new line hostage.

In fact, there were some rather literal interpretations of this: for some years, it was considered expedient for the EUR to propel all its trains into Colchester station with the locomotive at the rear, an unusual practice made necessary by the fact that, whilst the coaches were by necessity free to travel over the ECR, the directors threatened to seize and impound any Eastern Union locomotive that dared to trespass on to Eastern Counties metals. Complicated, uncomfortable and troublesome it may have been, but the early days of rail-roading can scarcely ever have been dull.

The branch to Bury St Edmunds also opened in December 1846, no doubt to the relief of the residents of Bury, who had often been promised a railway, but had had to wait some time for it to come to pass. This route, from Ipswich to Bury via Stowmarket and Haughley, was nominally proposed and built by the EUR, but under the aegis of a wholly different company, the Ipswich & Bury Railway (the I&BR). Designed, of course, by Bruff, it presented problems for the ambitious engineer, including boggy terrain near Stowmarket, where he took a leaf out of George Stephenson's book and built the embankment on a raft of brushwood, just as Stephenson had done at Chat Moss on the Liverpool and Manchester line.

As temporary and inconsequential as it sounds, the technique of using brushwood and woven hurdles proved to be inspired, as the lines built on this floating mat of organic matter are still in use, and supporting trains of greater weight, speed and frequency than the original engineers could ever have imagined in their most fevered nightmares.

Another problem faced by Bruff was the tunnel through Stoke Hill, still a dominant presence in Ipswich station today. Tunnelling technology itself was fairly well understood by this time, but the problem of water ingress was particularly acute at Ipswich, causing many difficulties in its construction. It remains a problem today, as the water still pours in – it is partly because of this that the track in the Stoke Hill tunnel is laid upon a continuous concrete slab, the conventional ballast and sleeper formation proving difficult to maintain in its correct alignment under the excessive flow of water.

The Ipswich & Bury Railway, at best only theoretically independent, was formally absorbed by its parent company in 1847, in the same year as the line to Bury St Edmunds was crowned by a fine red-brick railway station, designed by Sancton Wood in a slightly odd Tudorbethan-meets-Christopher-Wren style. Built on two levels, as the line occupies an embankment above street level, the Grade II-listed station is still worth a look, despite having lost a

A common postcard view, but one that shows Bury station well; it displays the two towers that marked a triumphant 'end of the line' when the station was in its original form as a grand terminus.

fair amount of its original glory. It boasts a pair of red-brick towers that flank the tracks, although when constructed the towers would have marked the end wall of a four-road terminus, complete with overall glass roof.

Now no longer a terminus, the end wall and two of the four roads have now gone, giving a peculiar air of space between the two platforms, and the overall roof was taken down in 1893; but standing on the platform, it is not difficult to see the station for what it is, a rather fine and still relatively unmolested example of an early railway terminus.

Onwards to Norwich

Whilst the EUR had succeeded triumphantly where the ECR had failed insofar as bringing the railway to Ipswich and to Bury, with the added advantage of the failure of the ECR's branch to Harwich, the full extent of the ambitions of those shareholders in Norfolk and Suffolk still remained unfulfilled by the end of 1846, namely the completion of a route through to Norwich. The EUR had not yet quite finished with their tame accomplice, the I&BR, as before the end of the year the latter company had submitted a further bill to Parliament – that of an extension to Norwich, following the line of the I&BR as far as Haughley, and then branching off northwards towards Norwich via Diss. Presumably the EUR felt that this proposal would be better coming from the I&BR than it would from them, although it must have been clear to all concerned that the two separate companies were effectively one and the same.

Nonetheless, the act was passed in 1847, and the same act also tidied up a few loose ends: it made provision for the 1847 incorporation of the I&BR into the EUR – a brief independent existence, even for a railway of the nineteenth century – and also for a branch from Bentley to Hadleigh, in Essex, branching off from the EUR between Colchester and Ipswich; this last would have been an EUR initiative.

Construction of the link to Norwich began in 1848, with a by now familiar roster of names – Peter Bruff and Thomas Brassey were once again in evidence, as were some familiar problems – Thrandeston Bog,

Thomas Brassey. Brassey was a prolific contractor with an international portfolio, notable for his generosity towards the navvies in his employ.

for example, a ten-foot-deep morass of saturated peat that gave Bruff just as many headaches as the bog at Stowmarket, requiring a similar solution to achieve a stable embankment across the fluid terrain.

In fact it remained troublesome until recently, works having been carried out in 2009 to stabilize the formation, using steel-retaining piles driven into the ground and a new technology called 'dry soil mixing', which apparently involves mixing cement powder into the wet soil, conjuring up an image of a monumental food mixer. 'Research provides a better solution' states the contractor's website, and no doubt it will be far more successful in the long term – but somehow it seems less heroic than Brassey's men, struggling in liquid mud and sinking endless weighted bunches of brushwood into the morass.

Even accounting for such problems, the progress of the extension to Norwich was much slower than that enjoyed by the construction of either the EUR or the I&BR. The main reason for this was that Railway Mania was beginning to lose its lustre, the national slide into depression – that proved the undoing of the great George Hudson – being felt here, too. Money was much harder to come by for the Norwich extension, no matter how much board members and shareholders alike desired it.

Nonetheless, by 1849 the line finally reached Norfolk, if only *just* – the first locomotive crept over the border into Diss on 19 January, and if it was only a small and rather dirty contractor's locomotive, well, that was better than nothing. By December of the same year, the line to Norwich was finally complete, although it had in fact opened in stages up to that point – as far as Finningham in 1848, and thence to Burston in July 1849.

Completion to Norwich

This grand achievement of a railway connection from London to Norwich, so hotly fought for, was celebrated by the construction of a rather austere terminus: Norwich Victoria. Built to a curious V-shaped plan,

its rather plain triumphal arch entrance was flanked by the two platforms under their wooden train sheds.

It was in fact Norwich's *second* railway station of what would eventually become a total of three, the first, Norwich Thorpe, having been built in 1844 for the Yarmouth and Norwich Railway; despite being a local line it nonetheless also owed its existence to frustration with the ECR's failings. This original Thorpe station was in a different location to the current one, which replaced it in 1886 – but not before the earlier station contrived to stage the era's worst single-line collision: in 1874 a series of errors, largely attributable to carelessness and poor communication, sent two trains into a disastrous head-on collision, in which twenty-three were killed and seventy-three more were seriously injured.

Triumphant though the EUR may have been to have reached Norwich after all their pains, their jubilation proved to be short-lived. In 1845 the little Yarmouth and Norwich Railway had formed an alliance with the even smaller Lowestoft Railway & Harbour Co. and the Norwich and Brandon Railway to form the Norfolk Railway, and the EUR had been making overtures to the board of the NR with a view to taking

BRIDGE AND STATION.

Construction of the first Norwich Thorpe station.

'Extracting the dead and wounded':
a melodramatic impression of the Thorpe railway
disaster from The Illustrated London News.

the line over. Due to the effects of the depression, and the dissatisfaction of the EUR shareholders at the rate of progress on the Norwich extension as a result, this particular ambition was abandoned, albeit not without dire warnings from members of the board of what could become if another company were to take the line over instead of the EUR.

A prescient observation this proved to be, too, as the Norfolk Railway swiftly attracted the attention of the ECR instead, who were fast becoming jealous of the traffic that could be enjoyed by the EUR (and which would, of course, have been theirs alone had they fulfilled their obligations in the first place). The ECR had managed to creep out towards Brandon by utilizing independent, unsuccessful railways and then just filling in the remaining gaps – a typically Hudsonian policy. A railway to Brandon now enabled the ECR to connect to Norwich via the Norfolk Railway – and thus the monopoly enjoyed by the EUR was snatched away, a loss they could so easily have avoided.

Even worse, as has been explained, *all* London traffic for the EUR had to come via ECR metals – so

although their route was easily the more direct of the two, their rivals now held a discomfiting degree of control over their circumstances. Indeed, at various points during this uneasy relationship between the two companies, the ECR effectively nobbled their neighbour by the simple expedient of refusing to sell through-tickets to passengers wishing to travel to Norwich from the capital, sending them instead via the less direct route over their own metals, rather than allowing a crumb of profit to be lost to the EUR.

Brutal though this policy may have been, it was not entirely uncommon – what we would now recognize as consumer rights were almost unheard of in the 1840s and 1850s, and many a competing railway company stooped to a similar level, hoodwinking customers for their own benefit. Even when the Metropolitan and District Railways completed the 'inner circle' beneath the streets of London, passengers were frequently pressured to buy tickets to go 'the wrong way round' to their destination – this was just to keep their custom within the territory of the company that had sold them the ticket in the first place.

Further EUR Acquisitions

2-2-2 well tank of the Colne Valley & Halsted Railway, Essex, built by Sharp Bros in 1849 for the LB&SCR. Seen here at Halsted, c. 1856.

Whilst all this was going on, in 1847 two independent railways opened to traffic that would both devolve to the EUR and contribute to its network. The Eastern Union & Hadleigh Junction Railway, although nominally independent, was developed hand-in-glove with the assistance of the EUR, in rather the same way as the I&BR before it. This alliance was part of a plan to thwart the ECR by building a branch westwards from Bentley on the EUR's route from Ipswich to Hadleigh, the seven-mile line gaining Parliamentary approval in 1846, and being incorporated into the EUR shortly after opening.

The second line to open in that year was the Colchester, Stour Valley, Sudbury & Halstead Railway (which must win some sort of prize for the longest company name in the region). Incorporated in 1847, the line ran from Marks Tey in Essex (already served by the ECR) to Sudbury in Suffolk, with provision in the Act for subsequent extension to Clare, and the construction of a branch to Bury St Edmunds, although it was several years before this latter addition came to pass. With the by now familiar troubled beginnings, the line had become the property of the EUR before it had even opened.

It did, however, act as a catalyst for yet another line, the Colne Valley & Halstead Railway, which ultimately connected with the CSVS&HR at Haverhill, although this latter company somehow managed to retain its independence until 1923.

The EUR Fights Back

Obviously the intermittent refusal of the ECR to sell tickets for routes that would benefit the EUR was a major problem, effectively restricting their traffic to an exclusively local base and making the EUR somewhat anomalous in isolation. This was a particularly bitter prospect for those who had fought so hard in the face of the ECR's apathy in the early days, when they were busy creaming off local profits without a thought for the people of Norwich and

Ipswich, to whom they had promised so much. Now the ECR's opportunistic arrival in Norwich was threatening the very existence of the railway that they had built for themselves.

To avert disaster, a bill was brought to Parliament in 1850 to give the EUR legally sanctioned running rights over ECR metals, enabling them to run their own trains into London, and thereby solicit their own passengers. Naturally this had a negative effect on what was already an unhappy relationship between the two lines. The ECR, ever combative, imposed heavier rates on EUR traffic over its metals, resulting in a fare increase of 18 per cent – a situation in which the modern traveller may well sympathize with his nineteenth-century predecessor. An attempt was made to resolve this problem via an agreement between the two companies to take a share each, proportionate to route mileage, of the total receipts – but it represented only a partial solution, and fares remained high, relationships remained acrimonious, and the passengers remained, in the most part, out of pocket and disgruntled.

This situation really became the thin end of the wedge as far as the rather feudal nature of the railways in East Anglia was concerned. The Eastern Union, with Cobbold still firmly to the fore, held a poor hand but was determined to fight until the last; whilst the Norfolk Railway was beginning to feel distinctly unhappy with its new masters. Even amongst the ECR board there were those who saw that this universal enmity and suspicion were counter productive, and rather than continue in a conflict that could damage all companies concerned, a small group of directors suggested an agreement with the NR and the EUR whereby the ECR would take over both lines, purchasing the two companies' rolling stock and effectively cutting the Gordian knot in which they had all become enmeshed. The ECR, predictably, refused to support the scheme.

The Eastern Union, meanwhile, in equally characteristic form, were pursuing the passage of another bill through parliament – once again, one designed to bring the ECR to heel. This was designed not only to settle the problem of running rights, but also to give the EUR some positive leverage over the misdemeanours of their recalcitrant neighbour. Passed in 1851, in a rather diluted form, the Amendment Act, as it was called, failed to give the EUR the running powers it desired, instead making provision only for the EUR to form agreements with the other companies – agreements that, if prior experience could be relied upon, were unlikely to be fully honoured. To this end, the bill also gave the EUR the right to bring disputed matters to arbitration should the ECR fail to honour any of its obligations.

Not surprisingly, the dirty tricks continued. The ECR instituted a road service for parcels traffic from Colchester to Ipswich in order to draw traffic away from the EUR, whilst also attempting to route as much Norwich traffic as possible via the Norfolk Railway. The Eastern Union, for their own part, sought to maximize their passenger traffic to and from the capital by instigating a steamboat service from Ipswich docks to Blackwall, conveying passengers thence to London via an arrangement with the London & Blackwall Railway, themselves no great friends of the ECR. Meanwhile the revised traffic agreement, provided for in the Amendment Act of 1851, was (not surprisingly) failing to produce results, and in response the EUR, flexing their new-found muscle, initiated arbitration proceedings against the ECR.

Financial Troubles for the EUR

It should be borne in mind that the EUR fought so bitterly because they were, in truth, in some considerable difficulty. The Norwich extension had brought in extra dividends, but not without considerable expense, and much money was owed by the company as a result, one of the major creditors being the contractor Thomas Brassey. Conceived at the very end of the period of Railway Mania, the line had been expensive, with strikingly opulent Elizabethan-style stations in red brick and stone, but had opened at the start of a period of national economic collapse.

Coupled with the financial drain of fighting prolonged legal battles with the ECR and the impact on receipts of that company's determination to hobble the EUR, the line's finances were in a poor state, the shareholders voicing their by now rather familiar

George Parker Bidder.

lament of low (or even absent) returns. Calls on shares provoked little response, and in fact a government auditor was sent in, an extraordinary occurrence at a time when government interference in commercial enterprise was not seen as 'the done thing'.

The arbitrators appointed to compel the two bickering companies to come to an agreement met in 1852, George Parker Bidder representing the ECR and Charles Locock Webb the EUR. As part of the process, a third arbitrator was required to oversee and mediate the deliberations of these two, and this third arbitrator was no less a personage than Isambard Kingdom Brunel himself.

Big guns these three may have been, but one did not have to be a giant of railway development to see the sensible outcome, which was announced in 1853, and in effect stated that the EUR should be granted reasonable facilities for through-traffic at its connection with the ECR. This took the form of an agreement that EUR trains would be 'taken on' to London over ECR metals using ECR locomotive power – so

the locomotives of the Eastern Union were still unwelcome beyond Colchester. Under this arrangement, scheduled times were of course to be observed, and of course in practice, weren't. The Eastern Counties routinely used the slowest convenient train to carry EUR traffic on to the capital, ensuring that their own trains offered the better service – and as a result the issue was immediately referred back once more to the arbitrators.

A Union of Two Railways

Ultimately there was really only one way out of the difficulties. None of the companies concerned was prospering, and none was benefiting from the curious games that had for so long characterized their relationships. The answer, as had been realized by those renegades of the ECR years before, was an agreement that would hand over the operation of the EUR and the NR to the Eastern Counties, this last being by far the largest of the three companies involved. Negotiations were set up between the two companies, the representative for the EUR being the dependable Thomas Brassey: not only was Brassey a major shareholder, he was also one of the chief creditors of the EUR, and could reasonably be assumed to have had sufficient incentive to get the best deal for the company.

The agreement finally reached was, in effect, the one that had been proposed several years before. Whilst the identities of the Norfolk Railway and the Eastern Union Railway would remain intact, at least from an administrative point of view, the operation of both lines would now become the sole responsibility of the Eastern Counties Railway. All locomotive and rolling stock would be purchased at a fair price by the ECR, as well as the steamships that had comprised the EUR's innovative solution to the traffic problem. All profits were to be divided, the Norfolk Railway and the Eastern Union taking one-seventh each, the remainder going to the ECR – not perhaps the best deal in history, as the EUR had a far greater mileage than the NR.

These strictures were formalized by Act of Parliament in August 1854, the passing of which marked the end of the independent existence of the Eastern Union Railway. This was something of an anticlimax compared to its rather noble inception, when the people of East Anglia, frustrated by the neglect of their region, resolved to 'build their railway themselves', and did so with dedication and some élan. Sensible the amalgamation may have been, but it was only to last another eight years. The counter-productive bitterness and competition that had characterized the business of these various railway companies could clearly not continue, and if the appointment of a government auditor had been unexpected, then the developments of 1862 would be revolutionary. In that year, the government would take a far greater hand in railway matters.

CHAPTER 4

Creating Order Out of Chaos: The Great Eastern Railway

Despite the growing influence of the Eastern Counties Railway throughout the 1850s – or perhaps, given the managerial attitudes that prevailed on the ECR, because of it – the chaos and infighting that characterized the development of railways in the region continued. This was against a growing backdrop of discontent amongst the shareholders of the myriad railway companies involved, all concerned that the bullying tactics employed by the ECR, and the constant battles between it and its neighbouring, non-incorporated companies, were causing harm to their share prospects. They may well have had a point, although with hindsight it is easy for us to realize that precious few railway companies ever represented anything other than a millstone around the collective necks of those who had hoped to profit by them.

Nonetheless, as rail traffic continued to grow and the existing partisan structure of the railways in East Anglia began to creak ominously under the strain, it was becoming increasingly clear that something had to be done to bring all these disparate and bickering elements together under a broader umbrella of co-operation. So great did this need appear that Parliament demanded that a bill for full amalgamation of the relevant companies should be submitted by 1861; this was despite the prevailing political attitude of *laissez-faire* at the time, which held firmly that

competition was to be encouraged, and that political interference with the railways at large was to be avoided.

This bill readily won the approval of the armies of disgruntled shareholders, and thus that of Parliament, who passed the bill at its second hearing on 7 August 1862. In so doing, they created the Great Eastern Railway, a new entity formed from the multitudinous struggling railway companies, which would hold dominion over the route miles of railway contained within East Anglia.

Or at least, *most* of the route miles. Nothing in the history of Britain's railways, created as they were against a backdrop of private enterprise and insolvency, could ever be quite that simple. There were a few notable exceptions, some of which coalesced in their own, highly individual way to form the Midland and Great Northern Joint Railway, a small but noble railway empire that ruled North Norfolk with a flair and individualism that is still celebrated today, and will be the subject of a later chapter in this book.

Despite the fact that this amalgamation was the obvious, and in fact the only practical solution to the chaos of railways that had previously developed, the birth of the Great Eastern was not without its problems.

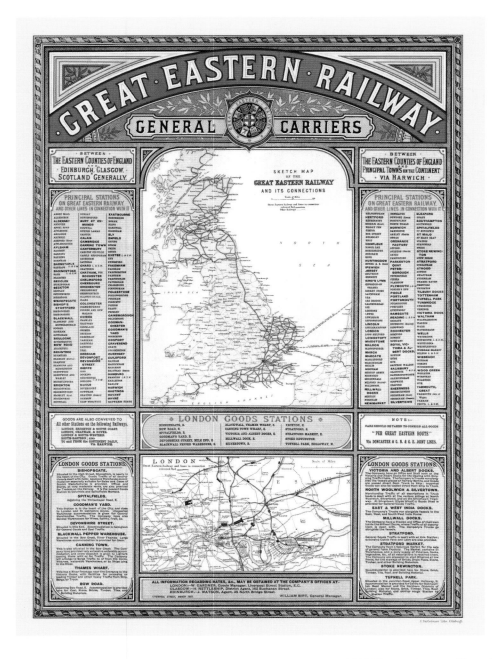

Great Eastern Railway poster.

The Formation of the GER

The composition of the new company drew together those two traditional enemies, the Eastern Counties and the Eastern Union. These two companies, together with the smaller railways they had absorbed, gave the GER a ready-made network stretching from the old ECR terminus at Shoreditch to Norwich via Colchester and Ipswich, plus a similar route via Cambridge. Yarmouth was reached via Lowestoft from Ipswich, whilst from Ely in Cambridgeshire, lines stretched to Peterborough, Wisbech and King's Lynn, from whence in turn tentative fingers spread into North Norfolk to termini at Dereham and

Three studio portraits of GER employees taken by Norfolk photographers around the end of the nineteenth century.

Wells-next-the-Sea. In the county of Essex, branches fed to Walton, Hadleigh and Harwich, to name but a few.

Supplementary to the two 'big players', the Act also drew into the fold numerous smaller companies that had retained their independence up until this point. Foremost amongst the 'B list' was the East Anglian Railway, technically still an independent concern, despite being operated by the ECR, followed by a list of railways of diminishing size and significance, ranging from the Waveney Valley Railway of 1855 that ran from Tivetshall to Beccles, where it connected with the old East Anglian Railway, down to the Lowestoft Railway and Harbour Co., a small concern that had been leased to the Norfolk Railway since 1846.

Many other concerns that were independent 'on paper', but which had in reality been absorbed into the ECR, finally relinquished their theoretical identities upon incorporation, including such half-forgotten concerns as the Stour Valley Railway and the old Ipswich & Bury Railway.

Being composed more or less proportionately from these pre-existing East Anglian companies, the ECR

was naturally heavily represented on the new board, even to the extent that the GER's first chairman was Horatio Love, the ECR's previous chair, who had held that post since 1856. The deputy chair of the board, James Goodson, was also an Eastern Counties man, and overall six members of the twelve-strong board were ECR men, the remainder being made up from the other significant amalgamated companies: the Eastern Union Railway, the East Anglian Railway, the Norfolk Railway, and the Northern and Eastern Railway, although the latter, at the time of the amalgamation in 1862, remained as an independent but co-operating company, not being fully incorporated into the GER until 1902.

This was due to the somewhat anomalous role of the N&ER during ECR days – the company leased their entire line and operating responsibilities to the ECR, whilst remaining independent as a financial entity, this position being maintained in the early years of amalgamation.

Horatio Love was not highly thought of on the board, partly due to his previous associations with the ECR, and was replaced in 1863 by James Goodson, who was seen as more confident

Another early study – station staff pose for the photographer against the backdrop of Buckenham signal box. Note the obligatory geraniums being grown behind the windows.

and forward-thinking. *His* deputy was Henry Jervis-White-Jervis, MP for Harwich and an officer in the Royal Artillery, who in 1855 had married one Lucy Cobbold – the daughter of John Chevallier Cobbold of the EUR. Known for raising his head above the parapet and voicing his concerns about management procedures within the board, Jervis-White-Jervis saw his concerns upheld and acted upon, a procedure that resulted in the ejection of various board members, including himself – which seems a rather unjust fate.

Taking Stock

The physical inheritance of the GER was something of a curate's egg, both in quantity and quality. Standardization was little known on the railways of the early to mid-nineteenth century, whilst the condition of locomotives and rolling stock could vary considerably depending on the impecunity of the company that had previously owned them. This became all too evident in August 1863, due to an accident on the Wootton section of the new GER. The accident was prosaic enough: a train bound for Lynn, composed of fifteen elderly six-wheel coaches with rigid underframes, struck a bullock that had strayed on to the permanent way half a mile beyond Wootton station. However, the results were disproportionately horrid: three vehicles left the rails, one third-class carriage being 'smashed completely to pieces'. In total five people died, whilst twenty more suffered debilitating injuries.

The coroner's jury attributed the accident to the poorly maintained lineside fencing in the first instance, and to 'the disgraceful state of the carriages used for the conveyance of the unfortunate persons'. In its turn this triggered a campaign of winnowing out and replacing life-expired vehicles.

The aftermath of the 1863 collision at Wootton. Extensive damage caused by a collision with a single bullock.

Furthermore, the cost of running this new network proved to be excessive, and a great deal of housekeeping was required to prune back expenditure and increase income. The GER in the early days was a financially troubled concern, and from the start was compelled to study its revenue-earning capabilities quite closely. It was apparent that the profits to be made from the East Anglian traffic (as opposed to that closer to and within the metropolis) were inadequate to support the new undertaking, and thus the GER was compelled to look a little further afield.

Coal traffic from the north of England was then being brought into East Anglia via Lincolnshire and Cambridgeshire, over the metals of both the Great Northern Railway and the Midland Railway, for further transhipment on to GER metals. Both of the above-named companies could also bring coal direct into London using their own routes into the capital. The Great Eastern, eyeing this traffic with an understandable envy, felt they could make healthier profits by cutting out the middle man and bringing down the coals themselves, using their own London terminus as a means to cream off some of the capital's voracious demand for fuel.

Starting tentatively, the GER proposed the construction of a short line from March in Cambridgeshire to Spalding in Lincolnshire, the hope being that, were the Act to be passed, they could force the GNR, with whose metals the new line would connect, to grant them running powers to the North, a suggestion that not surprisingly failed to secure the enthusiasm of the GNR. The latter company's objection was upheld and the Act was thrown out, and in fact the March–Spalding link, when finally constructed, was eventually built by the GNR, rather than the GER.

Undeterred by this workmanlike routing of their forces, the next overture on the part of the GER was to propose a new and wholly independent line from Peterborough to Doncaster. This rather ambitious proposal also fell foul of the GNR's objections, and likewise came to nothing. Back and forth went the schemes and counter schemes for many years, until an uncomfortable resolution was reached by means of a joint-ownership arrangement between Huntingdon and Doncaster; this was to be managed by the Great Northern and Great Eastern Railways Joint Committee, a rather cumbersome name for a slightly cumbersome arrangement – the immediate result of which was, of course, a diminution of traffic receipts for the GNR.

The relationship between the GER and its two Lincolnshire neighbours, the Great Northern and the Midland, was never particularly friendly, a situation that led in turn to the formation of the Midland & Great Northern Joint Railway, an almost entirely Norfolk-based railway empire (described in Chapter 5).

Financial Difficulties

While these rather unneighbourly wranglings were going on, the financial position was looking progressively gloomy. Attempts were made to raise funds via a further Act in 1866 by issuing debenture stock, but the uptake of shares was disappointing. An additional bill was proposed that would enable the company to raise £1,500,000, but this was rejected on the grounds that, even were it successful, the amount raised would have been insufficient – an unhelpful conclusion, but one that gives a clear indication of the problems that plagued the new company.

By 1867 the GER was insolvent, and an official receiver was appointed to oversee the management and operation of the network. Creditors moved in swiftly on the assets, identifying (but fortunately not removing) items of stock and equipment as their own property until such time as their outstanding payments were settled.

Such a situation was not what had been intended when Parliament pushed for the Act of amalgamation, and thus clearly something had to be done to dig the Great Eastern out of the mire – especially as it would have been evident that the mire was not entirely of the company's own making, given the failings and liabilities it had inherited as part of its rather dubious birthright. A further bill, allowing the issue of £3,000,000 in debenture stock, was passed in 1867, no doubt to the great relief of the directors of the GER.

A New Terminus

One of the more pressing problems inherited by the GER was that of its London terminus, the old ECR Shoreditch station, later known as Bishopsgate. It was deficient in both size and means of access, as well as being in an inconvenient location socially, if not physically, since Shoreditch at that time was a densely inhabited slum, unlikely to attract the custom of the better-heeled passenger. Some relief was obtained by routing a proportion of the surplus traffic into Fenchurch Street – rather as its predecessor, the Eastern Union, had done with its steamer services to Blackwall in the 1850s.

An atmospheric photograph of Fenchurch Street station in the late nineteenth century. Built by the London, Tilbury & Southend Railway, the station gave relief and a much more convenient terminus to the GER before the completion of Liverpool Street station.

Another view of Fenchurch Street, this time from within. Badly faded, it nonetheless manages to convey a good impression of a Victorian railway terminus.

The terminus had been built by the London & Blackwall Railway in 1841, and subsequently enlarged in 1854 to accommodate the traffic of the London, Tilbury & Southend Railway, a joint venture carried out by the L&BR and the ECR. The GER achieved access by leasing the L&BR, but paradoxically did not absorb the LT&SR, with whose trains it had to share the Fenchurch Street station. In fact, the LT&SR represented something of a problem for the GER, a line that remained stubbornly independent until 1912, when control was finally ceded, not to the GER, but to the Midland Railway.

This situation clearly placed limitations on the ambitions of the GER, who from the beginning were enthusiasts for the newly developing commuter traffic, recognizing its profitability and indeed becoming later known in its glory years for having one of the most efficient commuter operations in the country. For the exploitation of this traffic a new terminus was clearly necessary. As early as 1862 the directors of the GER were complaining of the limitations at Shoreditch, favouring the idea of a new terminus at Finsbury Circus, which was in fact the subject of a successful parliamentary bill in 1865, although ultimately unpopular both within the board, due to the precarious financial position of the company, and with the inhabitants of Finsbury Circus, for presumably rather different reasons.

Ultimately the present site bordering Liverpool Street and Bishopsgate Street was chosen. The proposals were ambitious: it would occupy a 10-acre site in the parish of St Botolph-without-Bishopsgate, and the compulsory purchase of the land granted by the Act displaced some 3,000 persons. The site had formerly been the location of the first Bethlem Royal Hospital, although having moved in 1676, it missed the coming of the railway by a generous margin. A bronze and enamel plaque, easily seen by a pedestrian today if they are minded to walk round the outside of the station from the Liverpool Street entrance to the Bishopsgate entrance, commemorates the Bethlem Hospital – but not the 3,000 residents the station displaced.

To reach the new station, it would be necessary for the GER to extend its lines for a mile beyond the old terminus, and pushing this extension through the streets of Shoreditch displaced a further 7,000 individuals, giving an indication of just how densely packed the area was at that time. By way of compensation – in part – to these individuals, a condition was imposed in the Act to provide a minimum of four trains daily – two incoming in the mornings and two more out at night – whereby workmen could be conveyed to and from their employment at no more than 2d a time.

This attitude was very much in line with the spirit of the so-called 'parliamentary' trains that were made compulsory under the Railway Regulation

Act of 1844. These were imposed upon the nation's railway companies by the government of Sir Robert Peel in order that low-paid workers might be carried in reasonable comfort and safety for no more than 1d a mile. The strictures placed upon the Great Eastern, however, rendered some of the tuppenny fares – such as that from Edmonton to Liverpool Street, a distance of some 21 miles (34km) – distinctly unprofitable.

The Construction of Liverpool Street Station

The decision on the part of the GER to build a vast new station came under considerable public criticism, being widely regarded as an exercise in expensive folly, all the more so given the financial troubles faced by the GER at the time. Large, proud and grand in the manner of most Victorian railway termini, it was designed in a Revivalist early Gothic manner by the GER's own engineer, Edward Wilson, and built in gault brick and Bath stone, an impressive, glazed, wrought-iron train shed covering its ten platforms.

It cost its owners £2,000,000, and also gave house room to the trains of the Metropolitan Railway (which opened in 1865 as the first underground railway in the world) and the trains of the East London Railway. The latter opened in 1869 as a joint venture between the GER, the London, Brighton & South Coast Railway, the London, Chatham & Dover Railway, the

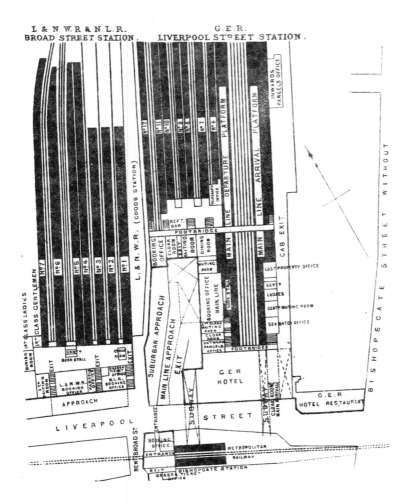

Liverpool Street station, prior to expansion in 1888.

Urban Expansion

Now with a brand-new terminus, the GER required brand-new services to feed it, and to this end it had been steadily spreading its tentacles out into East London and Essex in search of the commuter traffic it had been so keen to exploit. The approach to Liverpool Street was via the new Bethnal Green Junction, which later proved a useful springing-off point to give the GER access to Stoke Newington, Edmonton and Enfield, whilst a branch from Hackney Downs gave access to Clapton, Walthamstow and Chingford. Communication with Clapton, in its turn, made it possible to construct a branch that would feed traffic into the Cambridge line that had been a part of the GER since its formation, and a further branch from Seven Sisters to Palace Gates.

These lines were all proposed and constructed between the years 1865 and 1878, meaning that by the time the Liverpool Street terminus was fully opened, there was a comprehensive network of urban and semi-urban lines bringing traffic into the new station. In time this would pay dividends – in the conceptual sense if not the literal – as the GER were to become famous for their commuter service in and out of Liverpool Street, its speed, intensity and overall efficiency becoming a byword during the glory years of the 'teens' and 1920s.

And it was a market that was coming of age. The number of twopenny trains in and out of Liverpool Street had risen steadily, with twenty-three such trains each way per day at its zenith. In addition to these, the GER had instigated a tradition of workmen's trains for an apparently even less profitable 3d return, these being purchased in advance for a week's travel. The lines built out from Bethnal Green were also seeing an increase in traffic towards the end of the nineteenth century, as areas such as Hackney and Walthamstow became rich hunting grounds for development companies turning out scores of terraced housing for the newly developing phenomenon of the commuting blue- or white-collar worker.

South Eastern Railway, the Metropolitan Railway *and* the District Railway.

Overall, the new terminus was confidently predicted to be far too large for any practical purposes; little did its detractors – or possibly even the Great Eastern – know that by 1895 further expansion, to eighteen platforms, would be necessary to accommodate the flourishing commuter traffic the GER had been so keen to capitalize on.

Although still incomplete, the new station opened to traffic at the start of October 1874, sharing the load with the old Shoreditch station until the full opening of Liverpool Street a little over a year later, in November 1875 – at which point Shoreditch was closed completely to passenger traffic. The old terminus was not forgotten, however, being retained by the GER and ultimately converted into an independent goods station in 1881.

Extensions into Norfolk

In addition to the short-haul traffic in and around East London, the GER were beginning to turn their attentions to the north of the East Anglian region to Norfolk, where the spread of the railway network was somewhat slower than it had been throughout Suffolk and Essex. The GER would have regarded Norfolk as their own territory, a position with which the major companies in the neighbouring county of Lincolnshire, the Midland Railway and the Great Northern Railway, did not necessarily agree. We have already seen to what extent relationships between the GER and its two neighbouring railway companies were strained – and there can be no doubt that competition, rather than co-operation, was uppermost in the protagonists' minds.

Staff (and one civilian) at Brundall station around the turn of the century. The Mazawattee Tea signs were a familiar sight on railway platforms for decades; the firm belonged to the author's family until heavy losses during World War II forced its dissolution.

Key to this foray into North Norfolk was the East Norfolk Railway, an independent concern initially proposed as early as 1859 as a 25-mile (40km) long route from Norwich (Norwich Thorpe) to Cromer (Cromer High – Norfolk towns seemed to specialize in the duplication of stations) on the North Norfolk coast. Parliamentary approval was granted for the line in 1864, although it wasn't until ten years later that the line opened, in an incomplete state, as far as North Walsham. The full line into Cromer did not open until 1882, the reasons being, as ever, down to unforeseen expense and an overly optimistic estimation of profits.

The only thing for the ENR to do was to reach out to the Great Eastern for assistance, which duly came: the ENR, whilst remaining theoretically independent, was taken under the wing of the GER in 1881, giving it the impetus it needed towards its final completion in 1882. This acquisition included the branch from Wroxham to Aylsham, provided for in the original Act and completed in the same year. Modifications to the route meant that this branch could now join the GER at Broom Green in addition to the connection of the ENR proper at Norwich. This Aylsham–Wroxham branch, which finally closed to passenger traffic in 1964, now forms the route of the 15in-gauge Bure Valley Railway, described in Chapter 10.

By 1893, the Great Eastern had contrived to reach out as far as Peterborough, March and Wisbech in Cambridgeshire, and embraced the coast of Norfolk, with termini at King's Lynn, Hunstanton, Wells-next-the-Sea, Cromer and Yarmouth. That its influence in Norfolk and Cambridgeshire was not greater is due to the counter schemes on the part of the MR and the GNR, ultimately responsible for bringing into being the decidedly Norfolk concern of the Midland and Great Northern Joint Railway, the subject of the next chapter.

Growth of Liverpool Street

By 1884, the traffic harvested from the network of branches stretching out into what had now become the eastern suburbs of London, was pushing at the limits of the traffic that Liverpool Street Station – only ten years previously predicted to be nothing more than a costly white elephant – was capable of handling. It was, in fact, now working almost at capacity, handling some 600 trains per day, and it was becoming increasingly clear that, far from being impracticably large, the station was in need of expansion – and to this end the GER began to purchase adjacent plots of land to make this possible.

This would have been driven in part by the fact that the company's suburban ambitions were not yet quite exhausted. In 1891, a branch was constructed that ran from Edmonton to Cheshunt, whereupon it joined the GER route from Liverpool Street to Cambridge. Intended to capitalize on future residential development around Edmonton, which ultimately failed to

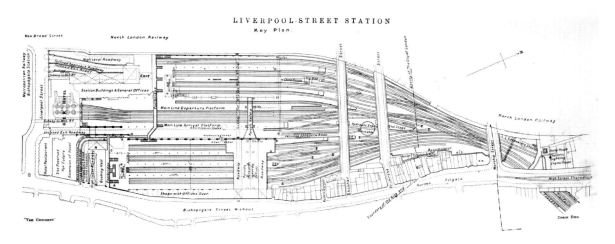

The enlarged Liverpool Street station, including the new suburban platforms to the south-east, as illustrated in The Engineer *in 1896.*

materialize to any great extent, the line ended up being rather an anomaly, seeing only light use as a freight route for fifty years after its construction, until British Rail found a use for it as part of its electrified route into Liverpool Street from Hertford.

With its suburban portfolio nearly complete, attention had to turn to the expansion of Liverpool Street station to accommodate the hoped-for increase in traffic. An Act of Parliament had been gained to this end in 1888, and by 1890 work had started on what had been termed the 'east side suburban' part of the station. This would provide a further eight platforms for suburban traffic, bringing the total up to eighteen, and giving Liverpool Street the distinction of having the largest number of platforms of any London terminus at that time. (For the curious, this record has now been eclipsed by Waterloo, which ultimately grew to twenty-four platforms.)

The new extension, pushing out from the east side of the station, was designed by the architect W.N. Ashbee, in rather more economical red brick compared to the stone dressings of the original building. It, too, incorporated a wrought-iron overall roof, and boasted new, clean electric light.

The newly extended station in 1896.

Lord Claud Hamilton

Hamilton was an ex-military man who embarked upon a career in politics in 1865, becoming Conservative MP for Londonderry. He subsequently became a Lord of the Treasury under Disraeli, before being elected MP for Lynn in Norfolk, then Liverpool, and finally Kensington South – simultaneously finding the time to be an aide-de-camp to Queen Victoria and a member of the Privy Council, as well as discharging his duties as chairman to the GER.

Hamilton appears to have been a good and businesslike chairman, achieving that position in 1893, having been a director since 1872. He retained the position until the GER ceased to exist as an independent entity in 1922, at which point Hamilton was seventy-eight. He died only three years later, at the ripe old age of eighty-one, but not before the GER had honoured his service by naming the first of the elegant Holden-designed S46 four-coupled express locomotives after him. This was No. 1900, which was completed *in* 1900, and led to the entire class being collectively known as 'Claud Hamiltons'.

By 1901, Great Eastern shares had climbed impressively to yield a return of 6 per cent, largely as a result of his dedication to the role. He travelled the network frequently, making notes as he went

Lord Claud Hamilton, the much-revered director of the GER, photographed during World War I. Note that the photographer has mis-spelt his name with a rather raffish but superfluous 'e'.

on details of operation and efficiency – clearly a man with an enquiring and precise mind, and the GER under his leadership showed a talent for doing the best with what it had.

No. 1900, Claud Hamilton, *the first of the successful class of GER 4-4-0s.*

The final suburban development undertaken by the GER was the construction of the Fairlop Loop, branching off the main line to Colchester at Ilford to join the Loughton branch at Woodford, creating, as the name suggests, a suburban loop from Liverpool Street and back. Opened in 1903, it was both troublesome and costly to build, and although not as unsuccessful as the Edmonton line, it nonetheless failed to deliver on its initial promise. However, it remained in service, a large portion later becoming the Hainault Loop of the Central Line.

The general feel of the Great Eastern Railway was very much that of a twentieth-century concern, notwithstanding its genesis in 1862. Undoubtedly the GER 'came of age' in the early 1900s, and it should be seen as no coincidence that this new maturity corresponded with the arrival of Lord Claud Hamilton in the role of chairman of the board.

The Light Railways Act (and Further Expansion)

Quite apart from the network of lines that had built up east of the City, during the early 1900s the GER also continued to fill in the more critical gaps in its East Anglian portfolio. This was helped by the passage of the Light Railways Act in 1896, an enactment that was itself due to an innovation of the GER, having been passed after the construction of the Wisbech & Upwell Tramway in 1882, a direct attempt to prove that light railways were a viable solution to rural rail transport. This is covered further in Chapter 9, which gives a short history of the Wisbech & Upwell.

Characteristic of this new wave of development were the Kelvedon & Tollesbury Light Railway, built by the GER in 1904, and the similar Elsenham and Thaxted line of 1913. These are also described more fully in Chapter 9, as befits their unusual and rural nature. Further developments included an extension from Cromer Junction to Roughton Road, to facilitate a connection with the Norfolk & Suffolk Joint Railway, a rather anomalous concern that was owned jointly by the GER and the Midland & Great Northern Joint Railway. Uneasy bedfellows these two may have been, but the connection with the N&SJR meant that a more direct path was available between Lowestoft, Gorleston and Yarmouth.

Henry Worth Thornton

The Great Eastern found itself the focus of some controversy during the early part of 1914, when the company appointed as its general manager one Henry Worth Thornton, who had the temerity to be an American – a fact that caused some friction in Britain at the time, since it was regarded as somewhat improper to source such roles from outside the United Kingdom.

Thornton, who looked every inch the American man of business, was born in Indiana and began his railway career on the Pennsylvania Railroad as a

Henry Worth Thornton, whose progressive ideas would revolutionize the management of the GER, although his appointment was regarded as unpatriotic by some.

draughtsman, before progressing through the ranks to the position of superintendent. The peak of his stateside career was becoming General Superintendent of the Long Island Railroad in 1912.

Thornton's arrival on the GER staff was at the instigation of Claud Hamilton, who was looking for greater imagination and dynamism in a general manager, and it seems that with Thornton he got it. He immediately rearranged the duties of the board, assigning to members separate aspects of the company's affairs to assimilate, assess and act upon, as well as introducing a pay increase for GER employees – although this last innovation became a source of embarrassment when the GER was later absorbed into the L&NER, as pay then had to come *down* again to bring it back into line with the other constituent companies. He also instituted a practice of having statistical data presented in visual form, a methodology familiar today, but revolutionary at a time when other companies

The Liverpool Street Memorial

Just inside the Liverpool Street entrance of London's Liverpool Street station, if the traveller looks to their right, is an impressive marble entablature bearing the inscription: 'To the Glory of God and in grateful memory of the Great Eastern Railway Staff who in response to the call of their King and Country, sacrificed their lives during the Great War 1914–1919.' Below this follows a tightly set and sombre list of some 1,216 names.

The memorial remains a striking element of the modern-day station, having been restored in 1990 after remodelling made necessary its removal from its old location in what had been the booking hall. This ensures that it maintains the same prominence to the daily flood of travellers as was intended when it was erected in 1922. Carved by sculptors Farmer & Brindley, the monument was dedicated by the Bishop of Norwich and unveiled by Field Marshal Sir Henry Wilson, Baronet, CGB, DSO. From 1918 Sir Henry had been Chief of the Imperial General Staff, after a war service that saw him play a significant role both within the British Expeditionary Force and later as military adviser to David Lloyd George.

Field marshal Sir Henry Hughes Wilson.

A smaller memorial to Sir Henry's memory was later erected adjacent to the Great Eastern war memorial, due to a remarkable and tragic circumstance: Wilson, who was Irish-born and publicly Unionist in his politics, was shot dead by two members of the Irish Republican Army on his own front doorstep at 2:20pm on 22 June 1922 – one hour and twenty minutes after unveiling the memorial at Liverpool Street Station.

were still scrutinizing long and baffling lists of figures.

Thornton would no doubt have had further revolutionary ideas up his sleeve, and ideas that may well have put the Great Eastern far ahead of its contemporaries, but the time of his appointment was hardly propitious. Whatever great visions the American entrepreneur may have had up his sleeve, they were soon to be overshadowed by events of international moment.

1914–1918: The Great Eastern in World War I

East Anglia occupied a location of geographic significance during World War I, its long coastline jutting out into the German Ocean, a name that was abandoned quite rapidly in favour of the North Sea after 1914. The proximity of the region to mainland Europe made it a useful staging post for men and equipment on their way to war – but the reverse was also true, and the coastline of East Anglia was now vulnerable, for the first time, to attack from the air as well as unwelcome attentions by sea.

The first British naval loss of the war occurred on 4 August 1914 at 06:35am, in waters off the Thames estuary. The victims were the crew of the *Amphion*, an Active class light cruiser of the Harwich Striking Force. She was sunk by a German mine, with losses of one officer and 131 ratings, plus an unknown number of German sailors captured from an enemy vessel that they had pursued and indeed sunk – the very same vessel that had laid the mines in the first place.

This engagement came about after the Harwich patrol, scanning the vulnerable waters between Harwich and the Hook of Holland, encountered one of the Great Eastern Railway's continental steamers abroad at about 10:15pm. Nothing necessarily odd about that *per se*, and in fact Holland remained neutral in World War I, but nonetheless, the Harwich squadron regarded it as worthy of investigation. Furthermore, the crew of a trawler soon reported 'people throwing things over the side' of the Great Eastern vessel, so the Navy drew in for a closer look – at which point, the steamer fled.

The vessel was, in fact, the SMS *Königin Luise*, a German steam ferry built in 1913 and pressed into service as a minelayer only a day previously, on 3 August, giving her a remarkably short war history. She had been cunningly disguised as a British vessel by being painted in the black, buff and yellow livery of the GER steamers, but due to the hurried nature of her engagement had not yet been fitted with sufficient firepower to defend herself, making her an easy target. Under heavy fire, the *Königin Luise* was scuttled by her crew and sank at 12:22, in what would have been a tidy and satisfying victory for the British patrol, had they not run back through the minefield on their return to Harwich.

The SMS Königin Luise, the subject of the first naval engagement of World War I whilst wearing the disguise of a Great Eastern Railway ferry.

EAST COAST AIR RAID JAN 19TH 1915.
A Hole 17' 6" wide, near Royal Train shelter, Lynn Station.

The aftermath of an air raid at King's Lynn (GER) in 1915. Note the reference to the 'Royal Train shelter' – a pair of Claud Hamilton class locomotives were kept for royal services, Wolferton station in Norfolk being closest to the royal estate at Sandringham. Both locomotives and station were maintained in immaculate condition.

The Railway Executive Committee

On the same day as all this excitement in the North Sea, decisions were being made in Whitehall that would shape the role of the railway network in Great Britain for the duration of the war – and indeed beyond. On that day, the railways were taken under the control of the Railway Executive Committee, a government institution formed in 1912 to facilitate the rapid mobilization of men and matériel in the case of a European war.

This piece of tactical forward planning was driven in part by friction between Great Britain and Germany at the time, with Germany making overt efforts to match the Royal Navy in size and strength. It was also driven by the Agadir Crisis in Morocco in 1911, primarily a dispute between Germany and France over colonial territories, and one that Britain wished to be well clear of; however, in the event, parliament felt bound by obligation to stand by the French. The German government backed away from the threat of war at the time, but it was clear to many in Whitehall that the situation was far from stable. Behind closed doors, the British and the French began to liaise in preparation for a potential war with Germany, and the Railway Executive Committee was one result of these negotiations.

Ultimately the committee was to retain control of the railways until this was finally relinquished under the Railways Act of 1921 (of which more in Chapter 6). Chairmanship of the REC was handed to Sir Alexander Kaye Butterworth, the chairman of the North Eastern Railway, who retained the position until 1919.

The creation of the REC meant that, for the first time, the British government could exercise direct and total control over the railway network in Britain, something for which critics of the railways had been calling for years, their political figurehead being William Ewart Gladstone. In peacetime their efforts had met with only moderate success, but in the face of war the railways temporarily surrendered their rather chaotic independence. It was to prove to be the thin end of the wedge.

Like so many engineering facilities during World War I, the GER depot at Stratford undertook extra work for the war effort in addition to carrying out the routine maintenance typical of a motive power depot. The overhaul of locomotives from other parts of the national network was carried out as capacity allowed, including some definite foreigners in the shape of a group of Caledonian goods locomotives and a pair of Belgian six-coupled engines from the Railway Operating Division, managed by the Royal Engineers, as well as munitions work and the construction of a hospital train for the Western Front. So extensive was the workload at Stratford at this time that an additional shed for the overhaul of locomotives was constructed to the west of the works in 1915.

The 'Jazz' Service

By the time of the cessation of hostilities in 1918, the glory days of the GER were drawing to a close.

The ever-dynamic Thornton still held the reins, but continued government control severely limited the potential for recovery, although company shares still returned a 2.5 per cent dividend, a respectable outcome under the circumstances. The last real hurrah was the apex of suburban traffic in and out of Liverpool Street, a market that the GER had been skilfully cultivating since the 1870s. Throughout these early years of the twentieth century this traffic had developed a reputation as the most intensive and efficient commuter operation in the country, earning the nickname of the 'Jazz' service on account of the bright colour coding used to identify first and third class at a glance, as well as, presumably, the bewildering speed at which trains arrived and were despatched.

Handling a staggering 107,500,000 passengers per year, it was an optimistic, postwar nickname for an optimistic, postwar service; trains were turned round within the space of ten minutes, and the now-familiar concept of identifying each service with a list of its destinations on the concourse was born as a means of speeding up passenger movement. Incoming trains would relinquish their locomotive and immediately receive a fresh one at the outgoing end, meaning that the approach to Liverpool Street buzzed with the activity of little blue tank engines in almost constant rotation.

Despite this commendable level of despatch, it was a service that cried out for electrification, as was happening elsewhere, most notably on the suburban lines of the Metropolitan and the District railways, as well as services on the London, Brighton & South Coast Railway and the London & North Western Railway. The GER, however, lacked the finances for such a programme of modernization, and so concentrated on doing the best with what they had. Their astonishing expediency, due in no small part to Thornton's visionary approach, meant that in 1920 the 'Jazz' service became the pinnacle of steam suburban operation, and indeed the final high note of the GER.

The following year saw the end of REC control of the railways, but the new Railways Act of 1921 meant that the form of the postwar network was going to be very different; it also meant that the career of the Great Eastern Railway, with its elegant royal blue locomotives, was finally at an end.

CHAPTER 5

The Midland and Great Northern Joint Railway

The pleasant village of Melton Constable in North Norfolk has a population of around 600, and in common with many of its neighbouring towns and villages, is unreachable by rail. Situated in a sparsely populated area, it boasts few major amenities beyond an industrial estate, and a noteworthy village sign in carved and painted wood that announces its incorporation of the ancient parish of Burgh Parva. Above this sign sits a creditable representation of an early twentieth-century 4-4-0 tank engine, resplendent in a vivid yellow livery that may appear fictitious to the uninformed visitor, no doubt puzzled as to the link between this sign and a quiet village so far from any railway.

And yet not only does it make perfect sense, but the carefully made and maintained sign betokens a local pride that still lingers. This is because for a period of over one hundred years, between 1853 and 1959, Melton Constable was known as the Crewe of North Norfolk, the area of land now occupied by the industrial estate having been once the heart of a proud and individualistic railway company: the Midland and Great Northern Joint Railway, or the M&GNJR.

To suggest that the line inspired loyalty and respect would be no understatement. The Melton Constable village sign apart, there is a thriving Midland and Great Northern Joint Railway Society, dedicated to preserving, exploring and interpreting the history of this most individual of lines. Furthermore the preserved North Norfolk Railway, itself once part of the M&GNJR system, carries the name of its parent company into the twenty-first century with pride.

For it was *that* sort of railway. It attracted that same fondness and loyalty that was peculiar to other Joint concerns, most notably the Somerset and Dorset Joint Railway, with which it shared more than a few similarities. This dedication on the part of employees and enthusiasts alike may perhaps be attributable to both concerns dancing an intriguing tightrope – too small a network to be anonymous and unwieldy, but too large to be remembered as the struggling branch line of weed-strewn track and rusting milk churn. Somehow they simultaneously inspired the fondness we reserve for the underdog, whilst also enjoying the rigorous devotion afforded to the old, pre-grouping railways. The Crewe of North Norfolk, with its engines resplendent in 'Golden Gorse' livery (the colour on the sign is indeed accurate) may be gone, but the memories linger on.

It may be worthwhile at this point to explain briefly what is meant by a 'Joint' railway. At one time there were some twenty-two Joint railways operating across Great Britain. Put simply enough, a Joint railway was a railway owned and operated by more than one parent company, usually for

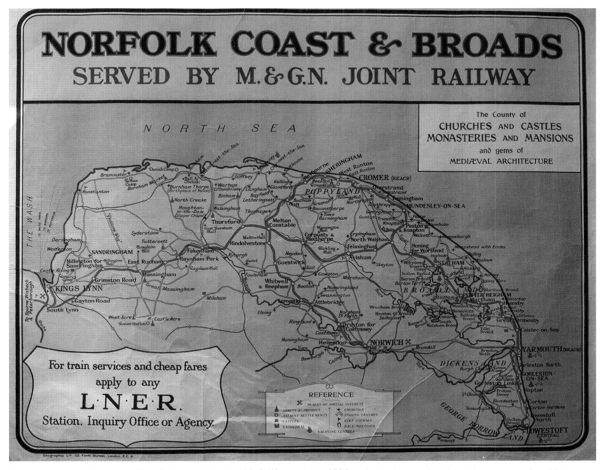

A poster showing the areas of Norfolk served by the M&GNJR, issued in 1935 and clearly aimed at the sightseeing market. Note that enquiries are directed towards the L&NER, whilst the poster firmly upholds the identity of the M&GNJR – this spirit of independence remained in place until nationalization in 1947.

reasons of expediency and the protection of mutual interests. In the case of the M&GNJR, the two controlling companies were the Midland Railway and the Great Northern Railway – which explains a name that at first glance might appear geographically alien to North Norfolk. Similar circumstances surrounded the Somerset and Dorset – it, too, was part-owned by the Midland, and Midland policy influenced the locomotive design of both railways – but in that instance the joint partner was the London and South Western Railway.

The M&GNJR was not even the only Joint concern in Norfolk. The Norfolk and Suffolk Joint Railway, which ran from Cromer to North Walsham, as well as from

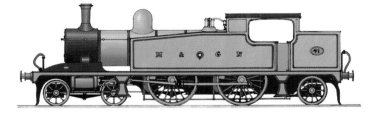

M&GNJR 4-4-2 tank No. 41, one of three built at Melton Constable and shown in later modified form with sloping tanks and Johnson pattern boiler.

Yarmouth to Lowestoft (although perversely, without any internal connection between the two sections), was co-owned by the GER *and* the M&GNJR – a possibly unique example of a Joint railway being in itself partly owned by a Joint railway.

The M&GNJR, at its peak, was the largest of all the Joint concerns in Britain, and held dominion over North Norfolk, edging gently into South Lincolnshire as far as Castle Bytham, and into Suffolk as far as Lowestoft, via the aforementioned Norfolk & Suffolk Joint – and this was by no means an accident. As the railways of East Anglia were being pressed into cohesion, the Midland Railway and the Great Northern Railway could see that the GER was gaining an unshakeable monopoly in the region.

The GER wanted to develop their own traffic from the north of England, particularly in coal – which, had they been successful, would have taken revenue from both the MR and the GNR. As both the latter companies had terminations in Lincolnshire, close to the Norfolk border, the obvious solution was to head off the GER by encouraging the independent railways in the northern part of East Anglia to team up – an inspiration that ultimately resulted in the birth of the M&GNJR. As a result, the early history of the M&GNJR becomes a complicated business due to the numerous companies concerned.

The Midland & Eastern Railway, 1866

Arguably the M&GNJR story commences with the formation of the Midland and Eastern Railway in 1866. This was effectively a Joint concern between the Midland Railway and the Great Northern, and the product of an amalgamation of two pre-existing lines, the earlier of which being the Lynn & Sutton Bridge Railway. Operated by the GNR, the L&SBR opened in 1864 initially to goods traffic only, with passenger services commencing in 1866. It gave running rights to the GER via a junction at Lynn, and was built to make a connection to Sutton Bridge, where there was an inland dock served by the River Nene, which held out promise for further development.

Work started in 1878 to create a new wet dock covering an area of some 13 acres, including a huge lock to the River Nene. By 1881 these works were largely complete, and a celebratory opening was planned for 29 June. However, on the 9th of that month, two areas of ground behind the dock walls dramatically subsided, which led to the disintegration of the retaining walls a few days later.

Needless to say, the planned opening had to be cancelled, and Sutton Bridge Dock was abandoned soon after, representing a huge financial loss for the development company – and a not insignificant one for the railway company too, as the L&SBR was not the only company drawn to Sutton Bridge by the promise of a new dock. The Peterborough, Wisbech & Sutton Bridge Railway received parliamentary assent in 1863, with a plan to connect the GER at Wisbech with Sutton Bridge, something that the Norwich & Spalding Railway had intended, but failed to do with their own unbuilt extension to Wisbech. In the event, the promised junction with the GER did not materialize, but the PBW&SBR were afforded access via the L&SBR junction at Lynn.

The second constituent of the M&ER, the Spalding & Bourne Railway, opened in 1866, its purpose being to connect with the Bourne & Essendine Railway, already operated by the GNR. The formation of the M&ER was thus intended to give a route for GNR traffic from Essendine through to Sutton. Whilst these two components of the M&ER were not physically connected, the gap between Spalding and Lynn was catered for by virtue of a lease of the Norwich & Spalding Railway.

The Norwich & Spalding Railway

The Norwich & Spalding Railway was the earliest of the many companies that eventually formed the constituent parts of the M&GNJR, its Act of Parliament having been passed in 1853. The intention had been to form a line from Spalding in Lincolnshire to Norwich, with a subsequent extension to the Fenland town of Wisbech in Cambridgeshire, already served by the GER. The full extension to Norwich was subject to a condition stipulated in the Act to

Waybill for goods transported from Walpole in Norfolk to Longstanton in Cambridgeshire via the Bourn & Lynn Joint in 1882. Longstanton is now served by the Cambridge guided busway. The railways operated amid a welter of such documents.

the effect that the Wisbech branch, which would give the town a theoretically important connection to the port at Sutton Bridge (*see* above), had to be completed before the line reached Norwich; in fact neither of these goals were realized, at least not by the N&SR.

Financial troubles, in part attributed to the Crimean War, severely curtailed construction of the line, and in the event only $7^{1}/_{2}$ miles (12km), from Spalding to Holbeach, were eventually constructed under the original Act, the line being leased and operated by the GNR. A further Act in 1863 allowed the N&SR to extend to Sutton Bridge without the additional burden of constructing the Wisbech branch. This last was finally realized through the construction of the Peterborough, Wisbech & Sutton Bridge Railway in 1866, which not only connected Wisbech to the port at Sutton Bridge, but also made a direct connection with the Midland Railway at Peterborough.

This rather tortuous set of arrangements meant that from a junction on the GNR at Essendine, Great Northern trains could now run into North Norfolk from Essendine to Bourne (B&ER), from Bourne to Spalding (S&BR), from Spalding to Sutton Bridge (N&SR), and finally from Sutton Bridge to Lynn on the GER (L&SBR), whilst those of the Midland company had access via Peterborough and Wisbech to the junction

at Sutton Bridge. Unlike the L&SBR and the S&BR above, the spoils of the PW&SBR went to the Midland. The line served both stations in Peterborough, in a curious circumstance where Midland trains would call at two stations consecutively in the same town, neither of which belonged to the Midland Railway.

East of Lynn

Now there were three significant companies with access to Lynn: the MR and the GNR, working in concert, could bring their trains into Lynn via their joint concern, the Midland & Eastern Railway, by using the metals of the N&SR and PW&SBR between Spalding and Sutton Bridge, and the GER with their

Norwich City station, the terminus for the M&GNJR.

line into Lynn from Ely. Now it was time for another new concern to join the party, in the form of the Lynn & Fakenham Railway. The areas of North Norfolk to the east of Lynn remained virgin railway territory until 1876, when the bills for both the L&FR and the Great Yarmouth and Stalham Light Railway were passed, this latter being at first an isolated concern with no connection to the rest of the developing network.

The Lynn and Fakenham line gained parliamentary approval despite opposition from the GER, and initially opened to Massingham only in 1879. The ambitions of the company were far from being exhausted, however, and subsequent Acts resulted in a line that, by 1882, stretched from Lynn to Norwich via Fakenham and Melton Constable, and from a junction at Melton Constable to North Walsham.

At North Walsham, an end-on connection was made with the old GY&SLR, although in the years intervening between 1876 and 1882, the Great Yarmouth and Stalham had become the Yarmouth and North Norfolk Railway, losing its light railway designation in the process.

As originally conceived, the GY&SLR was to be a 16-mile (26km) long line with its own station (later known as Yarmouth Beach), independent of those owned by the GER, to serve its lines from Norwich (Yarmouth Vauxhall, originally built by the Yarmouth & Norwich Railway in 1844) and Lowestoft (Yarmouth South Town, built by the East Suffolk Railway in 1859). In 1878, the GY&SLR gained parliamentary approval to extend to North Walsham, prompting the new company identity and paving the way for the connection with the L&FR.

The Eastern and Midlands Railway

It was by now quite apparent to the growing number of independent railways in Norfolk that if the GER

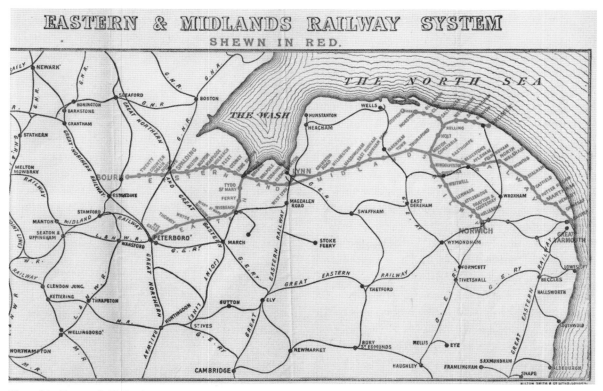

Map of the Eastern & Midlands Railway, soon to be transformed into the celebrated Midland & Great Northern Joint. The benefit of this strategy to the Midland and the Great Northern can be clearly appreciated.

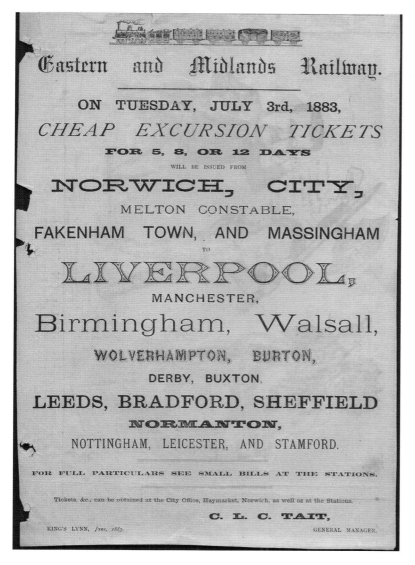

Cheap excursions from North Norfolk to the Midlands via the E&MR – a route that would become far better known for holidaymakers travelling the opposite way. It is interesting to note that this poster dates from 1883 – the train depicted and eclectic typography give the impression that it was printed thirty or forty years earlier.

were to be kept at bay, some form of co-operation was not only desirable, but necessary. The GER had a handful of lines stretching out to locations such as Cromer, Wells and Hunstanton on the coast, and Wroxham, Dereham, Fakenham and Swaffham inland, as well as Wisbech and Peterborough in neighbouring Cambridgeshire, all from their junctions at Yarmouth, Norwich and Lynn. It would have been clear to these companies, as well as to the MR and the GNR, that the absorption of these independent lines by the GER would be inevitable unless action was taken.

That action took shape in 1882, with the passing of the Eastern & Midlands Railway Act, which absorbed the Yarmouth & North Norfolk, the L&FR, and another small outsider, the Yarmouth Union Railway; this last was a short extension to the Y&NN that opened in 1882 and allowed communication between the Yarmouth Beach station and the quayside, already served by the GER.

Notably, as first conceived, the Eastern & Midlands Railway did not incorporate the Midland and Eastern Railway, a fact that seems almost deliberate in its ability to confuse the unwary via the subtly different names of the two companies. However, within a few short months the M&ER was itself absorbed into the E&MR, with the result that the new company now held a strong position in the region.

Naturally all these manoeuvrings were being quietly encouraged by the GNR and the MR, particularly given the level of influence the GNR had over the various companies involved. Not all, however, was plain sailing, as the E&MR remained an independent company, and its early relationship with both the GNR and the MR fluctuated somewhat. Furthermore, as time went on it became apparent that the fledgling company was not proving to be a profitable concern – not that this was an uncommon occurrence among railways – and by 1890 was operating under an appointed receiver. In the eight years since its creation, the E&MR had accrued liabilities amounting to £108,000 and unpaid interest on its shares to the value of £72,000.

Perhaps due to the problems caused by the independence of the new concern, it was decided at a meeting held in 1889 that the GNR and the MR should take over ownership of the western end of the E&MR. This was, of course, the section that was most important to the two larger companies and the section over which the bulk of their traffic was routed. The eastern end would retain its independence for a little while longer, although the difficulties that plagued the E&MR were in no way diminished by the removal of responsibility for the western end.

It was inevitable that the two larger companies would eventually absorb the entirety of the Eastern and Midlands, and this in fact took place in 1893, the relevant Act being passed in June of that year. In so doing, the Midland and Great Northern companies had cemented their presence in North Norfolk, and in the passage of the Act had formed what was henceforth to be known as the Midland and Great Northern Joint Railway.

The Midland & Great Northern Joint Railway

The new M&GNJR now provided a route from Bourne and Spalding to Yarmouth, 113 miles (182km) in total, with connections to the GER at Peterborough, Wisbech, Lynn, Fakenham, Cromer and Yarmouth, although in many instances (Cromer, Yarmouth and Fakenham being examples) the GER did not deign to share station facilities with the M&GNJR, meaning a walk for passengers unfortunate enough to be changing trains from one to the other. In so doing, a large part of the North Norfolk coastline had been opened up for rail traffic, paving the way for the holiday excursions that made up such a staple of M&GN traffic during the company's heyday.

Further to this, various alterations and improvements were in hand at the time that would develop the network still further. First amongst these was the opening in 1893 of the Spalding avoiding line, which, as its name suggested, avoided Spalding station for the benefit of faster through-traffic. Furthermore, the construction of a line from Bourne to Saxby was underway, which on its completion in 1894 gave the M&GNJR a connection to the Midland at Saxby, the connection of the two companies' territories being at Little Bytham.

The Norfolk and Suffolk Joint Railway

The Norfolk and Suffolk Joint was a rather curious anomaly – not only was it a Joint railway part-owned by another Joint railway (and in partnership with the GER at that), but it was in effect *two* railways, as the Cromer–North Walsham section and the Yarmouth–Lowestoft section shared no common junction, communication between the two being exclusively over M&GNJR metals.

Initially reaching out to the coast at Mundesley, the section from North Walsham was built in 1898, subsequently being extended along the coast to Cromer. Whilst giving access to the coast at Mundesley, Trimingham and Overstrand, a through-connection between Cromer and North Walsham was already provided (rather more directly) via the northern end of the GER's Cromer–Norwich line. The situation was much improved as regards the Yarmouth–Lowestoft arm of the N&SJR, which hugged the coastline between the two towns, calling

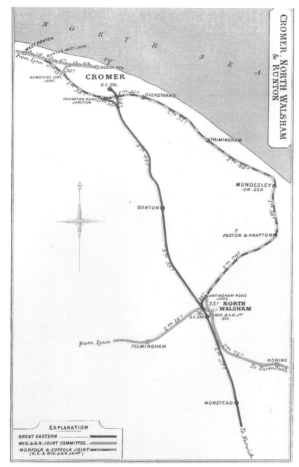

The Norfolk & Suffolk Joint Railway represented a curious arrangement between two uneasy bedfellows, the GER and the M&GNJR, making it a Joint concern part-owned by another Joint concern.

A further idiosyncracy was that the N&SJR also relied on M&GNJR metals to join its northern and southern sections together, as seen in this Railway Clearing House map of the Lowestoft–Yarmouth section.

at Gorleston (one station for passengers, another for goods), Hopton, Corton and Lowestoft, all major holiday destinations.

The GER, by contrast, could only connect the two towns via an inland line passing through Belton, St Olaves and Somerleyton, a significantly longer route. It worked in the favour of both companies to improve access to the coast between Lowestoft and Yarmouth, and thus the GER constructed the line whilst the M&GNJR undertook to offer no opposition to the line and to build a connecting curve to their own metals in Yarmouth.

William Marriott and the M&GNJR

By 1900 it can be seen that the M&GNJR had a small but enviable empire stretching out across North Norfolk. Primarily single track across most of its routes, largely due to matters of expediency, the sometimes intense traffic was operated on an electric tablet system, with tablet exchange carried out automatically using equipment built to Whitaker's patent. This facilitated faster timings than would have been permissible using manual tablet exchange, a consideration that was critical not only due to the

William Marriott, the long-serving manager and locomotive superintendent of the M&GNJR, whose exacting standards were key to the Joint's glory years.

at twenty-seven years of age, the youngest locomotive engineer of any public railway at the time. His career continued to develop in Norfolk until he became chief engineer, locomotive superintendent and traffic manager, all rolled into one – which could hardly have been a rest cure – for the M&GNJR, a position he retained until 1924.

Marriott was born of English parents in Basle, Switzerland, in 1857, but returned to England at the age of eleven after the death of both parents. He had been an apprentice with Ransomes and Rapier prior to his appointment on the Y&NNR, and clearly had a precise and imaginative engineer's mind; this enabled him to bring a number of innovations to the M&GNJR, which added greatly not only to the company's efficiency, but also to its rather idiosyncratic identity.

Marriott was an early pioneer of reinforced concrete – for example, the concrete works he established at Melton Constable produced what must be some of the first pre-cast concrete sleepers ever manufactured, complete with integral cast concrete chairs to secure the rails, as well as concrete station running-in boards, and even concrete houses for railway workers made from prefabricated components. It also produced a series of elegant openwork concrete signal posts that became a characteristic detail of the M&GN system.

Marriott also realized that, in order to maintain smart schedules with the graceful but rather elderly Beyer, Peacock 4-4-0s that made up a significant proportion of the inherited locomotive stock, standards of maintenance would have to be unusually high. So thoroughly was this policy carried out at Melton Constable that, as R.H. Clark notes in his extensive history of the M&GNJR, the Midland drivers who had double-headed a heavy summer excursion train and handed it over to a single antiquated 4-4-0 of the Joint soon had the doubtful smiles wiped from their faces when the Joint locomotive strolled effortlessly away under the heavy load.

Whilst the 4-4-0s in their unusual golden livery became synonymous with the M&GNJR, there was a plentiful assortment of other rather unusual types from its predecessors, some more elegant than others. These were gradually rebuilt under Marriott's

competitive nature of the M&GNJR's position in North Norfolk, but also to the running rights held by both the Midland and the Great Northern over M&GNJR metals as part of the Joint agreement.

In fact the Joint, whilst it could so easily have been dismissed out of hand as a rather provincial concern, took its duties very seriously, and in its heyday ran its lines with considerable efficiency and dispatch. A great deal of the credit for this efficiency fell to one William Marriott, who had started his career on a six-week trial working for the contractors on the construction of the Yarmouth and North Norfolk Railway. His trial was clearly satisfactory, because he began to crop up frequently during the works, and by 1884 had been appointed locomotive superintendent of the Eastern and Midlands Railway, making him,

M&GNJR Class A 4-4-0 No. 34, built by Beyer, Peacock & Co. for the old Lynn & Fakenham Railway.

watchful eye, often using standard boilers of Midland design, so by degrees the locomotive roster took on an almost-but-not-quite Midland flavour. The proportions were sometimes a little ungainly, and Melton had a tendency to go its own way in small matters such as chimneys, but the rebuilds were expedient and well thought out, and generally provided sterling service.

One such example is that of a group of 0-6-0 tank engines, bought secondhand by the Lynn and Fakenham Railway. Built by Sharp, Stewart and Company for the Cornwall Minerals Railway, they were repossessed by the manufacturer due to the original purchaser's inability to pay, and via the L&FR's ownership passed into the stock of the M&GNJR.

Generally they were regarded as being somewhat unsatisfactory, not least because their water and coal capacity was insufficient for the work they would be required to do, and so by degrees they evolved into some of Melton Constable's more interesting rebuilds.

Initially the locomotives lost the bunker and back sheet of their cabs in favour of a smart four-wheeled tender, making them into slightly odd tank/tender locomotives – but this unusual composition was really only the hors d'oeuvre. They were still regarded as rather slow for passenger work, so they underwent a somewhat more drastic transformation the next time they went into Melton works. When they emerged, they had lost their side tanks and been transformed into rather charming 2-4-0 tender engines, having had their four rearmost driven wheels replaced by new ones of larger diameter, with smart new splashers and new Melton chimneys, as well as new cabs, and the faithful four-wheel tender still following behind.

A few of their number were subject to an even more dramatic reconstruction into some well-proportioned

Sharp, Stewart & Co. 0-6-0 Treffrey, first of a fleet of eighteen such engines built for the Cornwall Minerals Railway in 1873, some of which were sold on to the Lynn & Fakenham Railway and subsequently rebuilt.

Seen here in M&GNJR days, L&FR No. 12A shows the first subsequent iteration of the CMR locomotives, with a new cab and Sharp, Stewart tender.

shunting tank engines, although surviving photographs of these would seem to suggest that the amount of original material in these later engines was actually quite small.

Even more remarkable was the transformation undergone by three Beyer, Peacock 4-4-0s of 1882 vintage. These re-emerged from Melton as handsome and powerful-looking 4-4-2 tank engines with a discernible Midland influence, new boilers to the MR pattern having been fitted, in addition to new side tanks, cab, bunker, wheels, and indeed possibly even new frames. Cylinders and motion clearly retained a connection with Beyer, Peacock, although quite how much of the original locomotive went into these 'rebuilds' is uncertain.

Nonetheless, a batch of almost entirely new locomotives, designed and built in the works of a relatively small railway company, was no small achievement for their individualistic resident engineer. Indeed, these three locomotives are regarded as being amongst the only four standard-gauge steam locomotives built in the county of Norfolk – although this point may be somewhat moot, as the shunting locomotives mentioned earlier as rebuilds of the old CMR engines bore scant resemblance to their former identities.

The fourth locomotive claimed for Norfolk was no stranger to M&GNJR metals, although not constructed at Melton, nor on the Joint roster. This was the diminutive *Gazelle*, built by Dodman's of

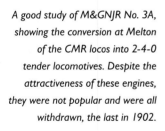

A good study of M&GNJR No. 3A, showing the conversion at Melton of the CMR locos into 2-4-0 tender locomotives. Despite the attractiveness of these engines, they were not popular and were all withdrawn, the last in 1902.

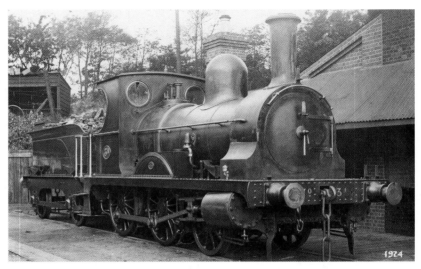

With later modifications betraying an obvious Midland parentage, one of the three 4-4-2Ts built at Melton Works from parts of the old Beyer, Peacock 4-4-0s sits at Cromer Beach station.

King's Lynn, a manufacturer of steam fairground equipment. Built in 1893, and claimed to be the smallest standard-gauge steam locomotive ever constructed, she was built to the order of William Burkitt, a local merchant who somehow convinced both the M&GNJR and the GER to permit the use of this dainty machine over their metals as a personal conveyance whilst travelling on business.

Equipped with an open cab and an extended footplate to accommodate a small number of select passengers, *Gazelle* was a 2-2-2 inside-cylinder well tank with odd composite wooden wheels of a type more commonly seen on coaching stock of the era. Coupled with her tiny boiler and long, spindly funnel, which made her reminiscent of a locomotive in a Rowland Emmett cartoon, her appearance would have been amusingly archaic even when new.

How long this oddball machine remained active in Norfolk is unclear, but by 1911 she had been sold to Colonel Holman F. Stephens for use on the perpetually moribund Shropshire & Montgomeryshire Light Railway. By a fluke circumstance, her derelict remains were later rescued and repaired by the military, who transferred her to the Longmoor Military Railway as a sort of mascot or pet. Here she found herself in the company of another locomotive whose path she must surely have crossed many times: this was one of the stately 4-4-0Ts purchased from Hudswell, Clarke and Rogers by the Lynn and Fakenham Railway. Which one is uncertain,

but with a suggested build date of 1880 it could have been either *Martham* (built in 1879) or *Great Yarmouth* (built 1881).

Whichever it was, it was less fortunate than *Gazelle*: worn out by 1930, it was used in later years for re-railing practice, and by the 1950s it was looking decidedly forlorn, though still sporting a Midland pattern boiler and Melton chimney from its later days on the Joint. Having thus outlived its sisters, it would have made an excellent candidate for preservation, but unfortunately it was broken up in 1953.

Gazelle, the diminutive 2-2-2 built in 1893 by Dodman's of King's Lynn for Mr Burkitt, and seen here at Lynn immediately after trials. Her overall appearance would change dramatically during her later life on the Shropshire & Montgomeryshire Railway.

The curious *Gazelle*, however, still survives, and after a long and colourful existence may be seen at the Colonel Stephens Museum at Tenterden in Kent.

The M&GNJR Freight Traffic

The freight traffic over the M&GNJR was largely agricultural in nature, not surprising giving the largely arable area over which the small empire stretched. Produce and livestock formed a large part of this, although with a large proportion of the Norfolk coastline being served, fish traffic made another significant element of operations – particularly if that traffic was headed north. This was because the Norfolk company held a definite advantage over the GER in that their traffic, thanks to the connections with the Midland and the GNR, did not have to be routed south-west to London before heading northwards. The same, of course, applied to the universal traffic of coal coming from the North into Norfolk, which had been at the root of the initiative to form the Joint in the first place.

Although the GER had their own routes into Norfolk territory, these took the form of individual tendrils isolated from one another, and as such they could not provide the same level of transport within the county that the Joint could offer. But the real jewel in the crown for the M&GNJR was the heavy holiday traffic, a direct result of their geographical dominion over an area blessed not only with an attractive sandy coastline but also the popular and expansive Norfolk Broads. Cromer Beach in particular was very much a 'holiday' station, regularly dealing with fourteen or more lengthy excursion trains in a day, whilst Hunstanton, Wells, Sheringham, Hemsby, Caister, Yarmouth and Lowestoft were all extremely popular holiday destinations during the first two decades of the twentieth century, all with their own heavy quotient of excursionists, and all dutifully served by the M&GNJR. Aylsham and North Walsham are attractive market towns with access to the Broads and remain popular holiday destinations today, and in fact much of the Joint ran through unusually attractive landscape, giving it a great advantage as far as tourist traffic was concerned.

This seasonal bonanza fed the needs of the M&GNJR well for many years, and for a time the railway was a profitable success, but the tourist trade was both seasonal and vulnerable to outside influences. Few influences could be more disruptive than war, and in 1914 the outbreak of World War I dealt a severe blow to the holiday traffic. Operation of the railways in Great Britain was transferred to the Railway

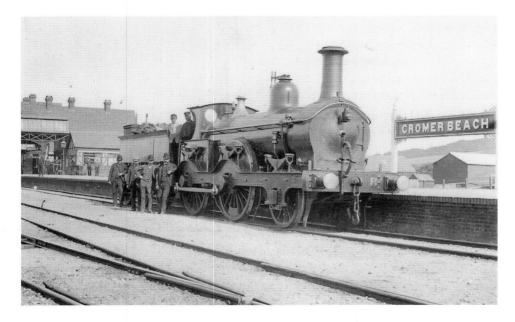

Cromer Beach station, with what appears to be a Midland Railway Class 800, built by Neilson for the MR c. 1870.

A Beyer, Peacock 4-4-0 backs on to the turntable at Cromer Beach in the early days of the M&GNJR.

Executive Committee, as described in Chapter 3, and the M&GN was no exception to the rule. Thanks to the coastal position of many of the Joint's lines, the company even hosted a fully armoured train, kept in steam twenty-four hours a day, seven days a week, to protect the coastline of Norfolk. Many employees of the railway left to enlist, leaving the company under-staffed whilst trying to keep up with the wartime demand for the transportation of men and equipment, which across the M&GNJR metals was heavy.

The works at Melton were pressed into war production, and carried out a diverse range of tasks in addition to the maintenance of locomotives and rolling stock. In a rather backhanded compliment to Marriott's regime, the Melton works ended up with the responsibility for the maintenance of many Midland and Great Northern Railway locomotives and vehicles in order that the other two companies might carry out more war work instead, it being considered that the facilities at Melton were superior in both provision and skill. This additional workload aside, Melton undertook machining work

for munitions, and produced track components for the prefabricated 2ft gauge battlefield railways that formed such a critical part of the war machine on the Western Front. The concrete works at Melton were also consulted with a view to designing prefab-ricated housing for a predicted crisis after the war was over.

Despite this productivity, the M&GNJR, like most of the national network, emerged from the war in poorer shape than it had gone into it. The intensity of traffic and the additional demands placed on infrastructure meant that a backlog of maintenance had built up and needed to be worked off. This situation was further complicated by the fact that government control over the railways was extended after the end of the war, in anticipation of greater amalgamation under what was to become the Railways Act of 1921 (this will be discussed in greater depth in the next chapter). The M&GN, typically, would manage for a short time to buck the trend here, too, the joint ownership of the MR and the GNR complicating matters until opera-tion was handed over to the L&NER as late as 1935.

CHAPTER 6

The London & North Eastern Railway

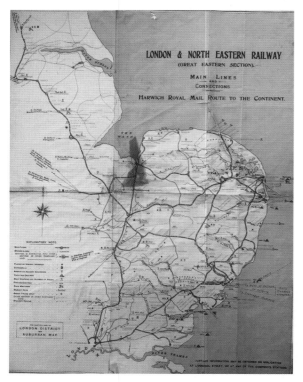

L&NER map c. 1921.

The railway companies of Great Britain were subjected to a major consolidation in 1923, known as the 'Grouping'. This was intended to cut down on the inefficiencies inherent in a railway system composed of multiple disparate elements, and increase the level to which the railways could be managed on a national scale, building on the period of overall control exercised by the government through the Railway Executive Committee in World War I. The result was the creation of four new railway companies, broadly corresponding to the four points of the compass. These would become the London, Midland & Scottish Railway, the Southern Railway, the London & North Eastern Railway and the Great Western Railway, the last being the only pre-Grouping railway to maintain its identity and earn a place at the table with the 'Big Four', as these new companies became collectively known.

The Grouping of the Railways

Control and efficiency were the driving forces behind this decision, the concept being the brainchild of the then Minister of Transport, Sir Eric Campbell Geddes. Geddes – and his career – is worthy of some attention. Born in India in 1875 to Scottish parents, he attended school in Scotland until being 'requested to leave' – for what precise reason remains unclear. He then travelled to America, finding somewhat improbable employment as a lumberjack before somehow gaining a position as a stationmaster on the Baltimore and Ohio Railroad. Upon leaving this

Sir Eric Campbell Geddes, Britain's first Minister of Transport and the man behind the Grouping of 1921.

latter position, he returned briefly to Britain, but soon after was to be found building light railways in India. He then came back to Britain once again, but this time for good, landing himself a job with the North Eastern Railway, within whose ranks he swiftly rose to become deputy general manager in 1911.

The advent of World War I supplied the next step in Geddes' remarkable career, as he was headhunted by the then Secretary of State for War, David Lloyd George (soon to become Prime Minister), and put in charge of munitions supply. In this role he appears to have succeeded handsomely, adding Director General of Military Railways to his already swollen portfolio, and collecting an Order of the Bath and an Order of the British Empire at the same time.

Clearly not a man to rest on his laurels, in 1917 Geddes was appointed First Lord of the Admiralty, despite the rather Gilbertian circumstance of his having no naval experience to draw upon. However, such was the character of the man it was unlikely that he would remain First Lord for very long. By 1919 a new parliamentary office had been created, and Lloyd George – now a much-celebrated Prime Minister – wanted Geddes to fill it: he was to become Britain's first Minister of Transport.

The 1914–1918 war effort had been heavily dependent on Britain's railway network, and over it the government had exercised a level of necessary control that had no precedent in the history of the nation's transport up to that point. It was clear in retrospect that there were definite advantages to having a level of centralized control in this way, and in 1919, as Geddes was settling into his new role, the government were preparing to hand control back to the independent railway companies with more than a little reluctance.

Efficiency was also a priority – the country was suffering from a postwar economic depression, and the prewar companies with their Byzantine complexity had held dominion over a network dogged with excessive costs, route duplication and loss-making enterprise. This would have been anathema to Geddes, who in 1921 chaired a Committee on National Expenditure, authorizing heavy (and unpopular) austerity measures that became known as the 'Geddes' Axe'.

Geddes formulated a white paper in 1920, proposing the amalgamation of the railways in Great Britain into five separate entities. This coalesced into a bill for the Railways Act, and received parliamentary assent in 1921. The Act, which extended the wartime government control over the railways for a further two years, now made provision for four regional companies, an arrangement that would become effective as soon as the government relinquished control of the network in 1923.

The fifth company that Geddes had suggested and had been subsequently dropped from the bill was intended to manage the London lines, but in the event the regional companies retained the London routes that had previously been the property of their constituent parts, leaving such urban companies as the Metropolitan largely independent of the Grouping. Only in 1933 was a further Act passed that created the London Passenger Transport Board, drawing these companies into full co-ordination.

The Impact of the Grouping in East Anglia

As far as East Anglia was concerned, the 1923 Grouping meant that all (or at least, nearly all – we are talking about railways, after all) the railway companies in the region would become part of the London & North Eastern Railway. Broadly speaking, apart from the GER, the L&NER also absorbed the Great Northern, thus removing at a stroke one of the GER's Lincolnshire rivals, as well as the Great Central Railway, the North Eastern Railway, the Great Northern Railway, the North British and the Great North of Scotland Railway, creating a new railway territory that stretched upwards from London to encompass almost all the eastern coast of Great Britain, a total of 6,590 route miles of railway.

From its constituent companies, the L&NER inherited a mixed selection of locomotives of decidedly varying levels of antiquity – 7,700 of them to be precise – as well as over 50,000 items of rolling stock. It also inherited forty-two sea- and river-going vessels, as well as an enormous number of road vehicles and horses – an indication of just how broad the operations of the railways were at that time.

The L&NER and the M&GNJR

The old Midland Railway became the largest single component of the Big Four, and the spiritual ancestor of the new London, Midland and Scottish Railway. This, too, had its repercussions in East Anglia, as it meant that the Midland and Great Northern, that erstwhile cat that walked by itself, was still owned by two separate companies after the Grouping. This prevented the M&GNJR being drawn into the fold of the L&NER, allowing it to continue its characteristic independence until as late as 1935 – although even then, this was accomplished by an agreement between the L&NER and the LMS to pass operational responsibilities wholly to the L&NER. This meant that on paper, the M&GNJR remained independent until nationalization.

A further peculiarity was that the London, Tilbury & Southend Railway, which travelled out into Essex from Fenchurch Street, became wholly the property of the LMS, thanks to associations with the Midland Railway dating back as far as 1912 – the subject of some disagreement between the Midland and the GER. The LT&SR had approached the GER repeatedly over a period of many years with a view to the larger company buying out the line, but since GER shares at the time were returning 4.5 per cent and those of the Tilbury line 6 per cent, the LT&SR shareholders were reluctant to sell out for a lower dividend.

The GER, on their part, generally dragged their heels, even when they were made aware of the counter offer made in 1901 when the Midland started to take an interest. They ultimately purchased the line via a parliamentary bill in 1912, despite problems associated with the dockers' strike of that year, which made business on the LT&SR temporarily very chaotic indeed.

A New Railway, A New Image

One of the most notable characteristics that came to define the companies of the Big Four during this era was the extent to which they developed what we would now recognize as their 'corporate image'. In this regard the L&NER led the field, appointing early on as advertising manager one William M. Teasdale, a man about whom little seems to have been written, but who quickly created a strong, modern image for the new company.

Influenced by Frank Pick, whose remarkable eye for design had unified and revolutionized the public image of the underground railways in London, Teasdale created a new logo for the L&NER that was the antithesis of the previous complicated, richly ornamented heraldic seals of the earlier railway companies. A simple eye-shaped (or *Vescia Piscis*, which translates literally, if somewhat unromantically, as 'fish bladder') border enclosed the initials LNER in a crisp Gill Sans font that was soon adopted as the universal typeface across the entire company's system. It was in fact retained after nationalization in 1947 as the universal typeface for British Railways as well, cementing an association between the font and railways that borders on the Pavlovian.

EVERY DAY

Commencing 25th August, 1928

and until further notice

DAY RETURN TICKETS

NORWICH and
Brundall and Lingwood

From or To NORWICH THORPE.	Return Fare, 3rd class.	
	s.	d.
Lingwood - -	1	0
Brundall - -		9

AVAILABILITY:

OUTWARD – By any train.

RETURN—By any train on day of issue only.

NEW AVAILABILITY CONCESSION.

Passengers will be allowed to alight on the outward journey at a station short of their destination on surrender of the outward half of their ticket, and on return may commence their journey at an intermediate station or complete it at a station short of the destination shown on the ticket.

CONDITIONS OF ISSUE OF CHEAP TICKETS ADVERTISED IN THIS BILL.

These tickets are issued subject to the Conditions of Issue of Ordinary Passenger Tickets, where applicable, and also to the following conditions:—

Neither the holder nor any other person shall have any right of action against the Company or any other Railway Company or person owning, working, or using any railway, vehicles, vessels or premises (whether jointly with the Company or otherwise) upon which such tickets may be available in respect of (a) injury (fatal or otherwise), loss, damage or delay however caused, or (b) loss of or damage or delay to property however caused.

The tickets are available only by the trains and on the days specified in the Company's notices.

If a ticket is used in contravention of these conditions, the holder will be required to pay the difference between the sum actually paid for the ticket and the full ordinary return fare between the stations named on such ticket.

The period of availability of these tickets will not be extended nor will any allowance be made for return portions not used.

Children under three years of age may travel free when accompanied by a fare-paying passenger, children of three years of age and under 12 years of age are conveyed at half fares, minimum fare one penny.

Passengers may take with them free of charge, at their own risk, articles for their own use up to 60 lbs. Third class, Furniture, Linoleum, Musical Instruments, Cycles, Mail Carts, Typewriters and other similar articles are excepted from this arrangement.

In those cases where the rail journey is not continuous through tickets do not include the cost of conveyance from one station to another in the same town.   (Z2)

Tickets, available from Norwich only, can also be obtained in advance at :—
PICKFORDS, Ltd., 74, Prince of Wales Road, Norwich.

London, August, 1928.

L·N·E·R

9482/8/28—6,000   PRINTED AT THE COMPANY'S WORKS, STRATFORD.   No. 4886

Early L&NER poster advertising return fares from Norwich, Brundall and Lingwood. Although pre-dating the rollout of Gill Sans across the region, the poster already shows a fresh and distinctive approach to design.

The overall image was sleek, pared back and modern, this being emphasized by enticing new posters in the Art Deco style. The realist styles of the Edwardian era were therefore replaced by bold impressionism and bright colours to suggest a railway world in which everything was clean and bright, trains were fast and efficient, passengers were happy, and the sun was always, always shining.

Such was the power of the new image that in many respects it can be said to have worked – certainly the abiding image we have now of the Big Four companies is that established in our minds by the marketing of the time. But this is a romance of the railway poster, not of the railways themselves. The posters held their greatest resonance for those who travelled on the mainline routes – London to Scotland,

Locomotives and Stock

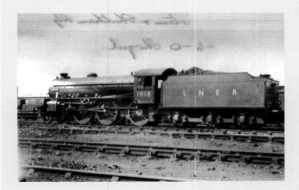

L&NER Thompson B1 No. 1018. The mixed-traffic B1s were used extensively throughout the East Anglian region.

The L&NER, at its formation, naturally inherited a great deal of stock from its constituent companies, and whilst these companies had made considerable strides in standardization on their own part, it was by no means a unified stock that passed to the new company. Across East Anglia, the old GER types were still very much in evidence, and some stalwarts were to remain a familiar sight long after the L&NER had itself become a memory. A striking example was the hard-working J15 (GER Y14) six-coupled tender locomotive; these were still in regular service in rural areas until the early 1960s, despite many having been built before the end of the nineteenth century.

Nonetheless, a company that wished to sell itself as a streamlined, clean, efficient and above all *modern* transport operator needed more than a few beguiling posters to do so, and the L&NER was fortunate in this regard in its appointment of its first chief mechanical engineer (later Sir) Herbert Nigel Gresley.

Gresley produced a series of new locomotives that have almost become the epitome of locomotive design during the inter-war period, many of them having become icons in their own right; the two record breakers were A3 no. 4472 *Flying Scotsman* and the streamlined A4 no. 4468 *Mallard*, arguably the most famous steam locomotives in Britain. He had been 'acquired' by the L&NER at the Grouping, having formerly been CME for the Great Northern Railway after Henry A. Ivatt; here he designed a series of workmanlike locomotives that not only demonstrated Ivatt's influence over the younger engineer, but which clearly presage his later efforts for the L&NER.

An interesting footplate view of the Mid-Suffolk Light Railway J15, No. 65447.

Stylistically and mechanically elegant, his locomotives and passenger stock became the perfect complement to the image the L&NER wished to present, the streamlined A4s in particular embodying the new ideals of sleek, smooth design and, more importantly, speed – even if not all of them were capable of the same galloping feats as *Mallard*. For the traveller in East Anglia, the Gresley-designed 4-6-0 B17s were a much more familiar sight than the headline-grabbing A3s and A4s, and even received a touch of the 1930s glamour themselves; a handful were turned out in streamlined casings, giving them the appearance of slightly diluted A4s, one such being No. 2859, *East Anglian*.

Striking they may have been, but the streamlining was almost purely cosmetic, some of the old GER diehards on the staff muttering that a better performance was put up by the old 4-4-0 Claud Hamilton class in their glory days than was achieved by the new-look B17s. Not that the 4-4-0s were absent – most remained in service, being progressively rebuilt under Gresley. In fact two of them, nos 8783 and 8787, were reserved exclusively for hauling the royal train to Wolverton, and both locomotives and station were maintained in perpetually immaculate condition, Wolverton being the nearest station for the royal Sandringham estate.

for example – and those for whom the L&NER was a 'holiday' railway, transporting them to popular destinations on the east coast during the summer months.

For those making routine journeys on the smaller lines and branches, however, the railway scene had not changed appreciably in many years, except perhaps in terms of staff uniforms and liveries. These lines were a long way away from the streamlined glamour of the new image, the locomotives and rolling stock of early GER parentage still going about their daily business, as indeed they would continue to do for many years to come.

1926: The General Strike

The spring of 1926 proved to be a difficult time for all the Big Four companies, and indeed the country as a whole, thanks to a combination of problems that had their root in the immediate aftermath of World War I. Most of these issues centred round the coal mining industry, which had been subjected to unusually heavy demands during the war, as well as suffering a significant loss of export revenue as an inevitable consequence of conflict in Europe.

The postwar result of this was that the industry emerged in dire need of investment, many seams being dangerously overworked, whilst the domestic market, finding its home supplies compromised,

looked to the continent for imported coal to make up the shortfall, putting further pressure on an ailing industry. This was compounded by the reintroduction of the gold standard as a benchmark for currency exchange, a decision that crippled the profitability of the export market, whether the product was coal or anything else.

The response of the coal industry to this crisis was to impose heavy wage cuts on the labour force, along with significantly extended working hours – a decision finely calculated to attract the condemnation of the Trades Union Congress, who found their appeals to the government to step in and pass a law prohibiting such measures falling upon deaf ears.

Negotiations having stalled, the TUC called a general strike in support of the miners. Although termed a 'general' strike, the intended protagonists were workers from the heavy industries – as well as miners, such trades as ironworkers, steelworkers and dockworkers were called out, in addition to printworkers and transport workers – including, of course, railwaymen. Strike action began at midnight on 3 May 1926, and lasted for ten days.

The attitude of the L&NER to the strikers within their own ranks was to treat the situation as an internal problem, rather than one with a wider political agenda. It was made clear that employees who struck would be regarded as being in breach of the terms of their employment, having as they did no direct issue with the L&NER itself. It was further made clear that the predicted downturn in traffic after the strike was over would have an impact on employment figures, and of those employees to be retained, preference would be given to those who had remained at work.

Operations during the Strike

During the ten days of the strike, the L&NER managed to operate services at 15 per cent of normal capacity, the labour force that had opted to remain at work being supplemented by enthusiastic volunteer labour, a concept that today seems rather alarming. Specific instructions were issued relating to the operation of trains driven and fired by amateurs, and their direction by signalmen – who would also frequently be amateurs. Hand signalling and extreme caution was the order of the day, whilst speeds were cut to a minimum.

The miracle is that it worked at all, and that no serious mishaps occurred as a result of such a haphazard method of operation, far more reminiscent of the early, gung-ho era of rail travel than the staid and responsible years of the 1920s. Such accidents that did occur, such as the derailment near Newcastle of an L&NER train bound for Edinburgh, were often due to deliberate sabotage by political activists.

Many of the day-to-day matters of the L&NER during this period can be found in the *LNER News*, an internal publication distributed throughout the system during the strike. As well as documenting traffic percentages and other items of general operational interest, propaganda was a significant part of the remit, as it documents support for the company – 'messages of loyalty have been received from various points on the LNER' – as well as human-interest news: 'Our volunteers are demons for work, but last night they gave evidence of other talents.' Apparently a group at King's Cross organized an informal 'sing-song and dance' after the day's work, a luxury afforded by the fact that all traffic wisely stopped before dark during the strike.

The Volunteer Force

The strike also drew some cultural lines that are perceptible within the pages of the *LNER News*. The announcement that 'Brigadier General Rawson has been working as a guard on the LNER at Hitchin' floats on the printed page as a curious but socially informative non-sequitur, whilst the item below it recounts how one volunteer, who drove 'with expert knowledge and experience…the Liverpool Street–Yarmouth train' brought fifty of his friends with him to help at Liverpool Street. The enthusiastic volunteer was the Honourable Lionel Guest OBE, businessman, politician and Old Etonian, although at some point

Volunteers on the L&NER during the 1926 General Strike, transhipping coal from the standard-gauge to the narrow-gauge wagons of the Southwold Railway at Halesworth.

in his career he had, indeed, trained as a locomotive driver. Who his friends were is not recorded, but it would be fair to assume that they were drawn from similar societal strata.

There was thus something rather carefree and dilettante about the volunteer force, almost as if the railways were being run by the characters of a P.G. Wodehouse novel. One passenger commented that it was such a pleasure to hear a refined *Oxford* accent announcing train departures. In fairness, the volunteers managed to run the railways with minimal training and few mishaps, and although only a skeleton service, from the 148 trains run over the entire L&NER system on the first day of the strike, volunteer action had increased this number to an impressive 1,245 on the ninth day.

Ultimately, from the political viewpoint of the workers, the General Strike was to prove ineffectual. An attempt to picket motor lorries outside the London docks was effectively broken by the military, and the TUC felt that they were losing control of the strike, with large numbers of workers beginning to return to employment. An attempt to agree terms with the government was met with a firm rebuttal, and the strike was called off on 12 May.

It still took some days for everything to return to normal – the chief general manager of the L&NER wrote from the central office at King's Cross urging the volunteers to remain in service 'until the matter has been brought to a satisfactory conclusion', the matter of course being the thorny one of whether or not the strikers should be allowed to return to work. Ultimately those who did return were re-engaged without a reduction in pay or extension of hours – but true to their word, the company still regarded their action as being directed unjustly against the L&NER, rather than viewing it in the wider political context of being in sympathy with the miners. Thus their re-engagement came with the caveat that 'the Company reserves any rights they possess in consequence of your having broken your contract of service.'

The strike remained a controversial subject among railway workers for many years to come, and those who had remained loyal to the company during the turmoil often found it wisest to remain

Whitemoor Marshalling Yard

A significant innovation made by the L&NER in Cambridgeshire was the development in 1929 of the Whitemoor marshalling yard at March. Designed upon ultra-modern principles, this was a 'hump' yard, in which an artificial gradient at the mouth of the yard allowed freight wagons to travel into the yard by gravity, relying on their own inertia to propel them into their allocated sidings rather than requiring locomotives to manoeuvre them into position.

These movements were controlled by shunters or 'splitters' – men whose job it was to break up the incoming trains into separate wagons or groups of wagons for redistribution – and also by the control tower, overlooking the entire yard; this had control over the route the wagons would take, and their speed, using remotely operated retarders that would check the progress of the wagons running down from the 'hump'. This was skilled work, requiring fine judgement, as the wagons could only be slowed once within the yard. A wagon that stopped short of its object would need to be propelled there by a locomotive, with commensurate impact on the efficiency of the yard.

And it *was* efficient. In the context of a railway network peppered with hundreds of old-fashioned shunting yards, Whitemoor increased the speed and reduced the cost of freight handling significantly, frequently 'cutting', reassembling and dispatching in excess of 200 trains a day. By the mid-1930s, Whitemoor Yard had grown to accommodate some eighty-four separate roads within a site covering some 250 acres of Cambridgeshire fenland, and was second only to the largest marshalling yard in Europe. It was a new model of freight handling that the British railway network desperately needed, its freight operations having hardly changed since the mid-nineteenth century.

quiet about it. The railways maintained a tradition of long service, and with long service came a long collective memory.

As regards the miners, there was little comfort from their efforts. Although many were left unemployed, many returned to work, but were punished for their actions by reduced pay and extended hours, the very situation they had struck to avoid. It was generally felt within the industry that their efforts had all been for nought.

Modernization of the Commuter Services

The suburban services in and out of Liverpool Street remained intensive under the administration of the L&NER, but whereas the expedient GER had sought to achieve the best possible results with what was available, its successor was thinking in more progressive terms. Electrification of the busy commuter lines was clearly the way forwards,

meaning not only a considerable investment in terms of new equipment but also significant revisions in the track layout in the vicinity of Liverpool Street station.

The L&NER decided on a system of power transmission using overhead wires, using a 1500v DC supply. One of the first commuter routes to receive the new technology ran between Liverpool Street and Shenfield, for which new electric multiple units were designed by the L&NER. Ninety-two of these were constructed in total, six of them built and delivered before the outbreak of war, although these were initially put into storage, as the work to electrify the line would not be completed until 1949.

As delivered, these units showed an interesting departure for the L&NER by being outshopped in a blue and cream livery, quite different from the characteristic apple green of the company's steam passenger locomotives, and foreshadowing the adoption of the blue and grey livery of BR in the 1970s.

The L&NER AM6 EMUs (later BR Class 306) had long working lives. Unit 031 is seen here at Romford in 1981.

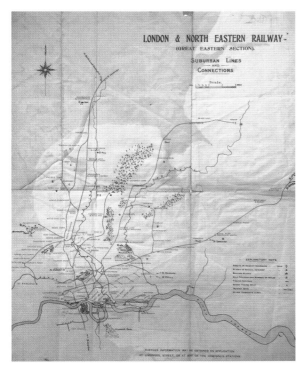

The London suburban network of the L&NER. Most of this had been constructed by the GER prior to World War I.

However, before these units – designated Class AM6 by the L&NER – made their appearance on the public stage, they had been repainted in a simple green livery.

They finally emerged into passenger service in the postwar years, after their parent company had disappeared into the nationalized network, but nonetheless quietly clocked up some impressive service lifetimes. The last examples were withdrawn as late as 1981, having been equipped with on-board transformers and rectifiers to make them compatible with the later 25kV standard for overhead power.

1939–1945: The L&NER in World War II

As had been the case with the Great Eastern Railway before it, the glorious heyday of the L&NER was cut short in 1939 by the advent of another European war. Once again the railways of East Anglia would have an important role to play, but the L&NER had already

Making Way for the Electric Age

The Great Eastern's famous steam-hauled 'Jazz' service of the late 'teens and 1920s had made use of a complex mesh of level crossovers and junctions to channel the eighteen platform roads of the terminus into the main running lines in and out of the station and to transfer the endless swarm of small tank engines to and from their trains. It worked well at the time, but the new electric trains planned by the L&NER were going to require a very different sort of layout.

The prevalence of flat junctions at the entrance to a busy commuter station meant that trains could frequently be delayed in their approach by others crossing their path, extending schedule times and introducing inefficiency into the service. The use of flying junctions, where one route can pass above or below another, removes this issue, but none existed in the approaches to Liverpool Street station in the early 1920s. This was solved by the construction of a new high-level line between Manor Park and Ilford, access to which was achieved by means of a rearrangement of the running lines at Stratford. New stations were constructed at Manor Park, Forest Gate and Maryland, but ultimately the project – at least under the auspices of the L&NER – was doomed, because by 1939, international affairs suddenly took a much higher priority than any domestic infrastructure project.

played an important humanitarian role before war had even been declared.

On 2 December 1938, there docked at Harwich the first of a number of steamers that were soon to arrive from the continent. Many of the passengers from the steamer entrained at Harwich for Liverpool Street, although some remained for the time being, lodging at the nearby Dovercourt Holiday Camp.

They weren't on holiday, though. This was the start of the *Kindertransport*, and the 200 steamer passengers on that day were unaccompanied children from a Jewish orphanage in Berlin that had been destroyed during the anti-semitic pogrom of *Kristallnacht*. All told, some 10,000 Jewish children were evacuated from Europe before the outbreak of war, most of them arriving at Harwich and travelling on to new homes in Britain by train. Their journeys are commemorated today by a bronze statue outside Liverpool Street station. The work of sculptor Frank Meisler, it was unveiled in 2006.

Reprise of the REC

Like the first war, it was evident that conflict was coming, although unlike the first war, this fact was rather more widely apparent. In September 1938 the government revived the old Railway Executive Committee, reprising its role to undertake control of the railway network in the case of war. The REC would be responsible for the operations of all the Big Four companies as well as the London Passenger Transport Board (later to become London Transport), not to mention such die-hard oddballs as the Kent and East Sussex Railway and the moribund Shropshire & Montgomeryshire Railway – and in East Anglia, even the diminutive King's Lynn Docks & Railway Company.

In order to carry out this role in safety, whilst still maintaining close communication with government, the REC was given a rather splendidly suitable wartime hideout – the platforms of the disused Down Street tube station (on today's Piccadilly Line) were converted into a network of subterranean offices from which the above-ground rail network could be administered.

War Traffic in East Anglia

If anything, the railways of East Anglia were busier during the second war than they had been during the first. Critically, the geography of this war was different – France and the Netherlands soon fell to Nazi occupation, and thus the east coast faced the enemy across a mere 30 miles or so of water. The coastline became of far greater strategic importance than had ever been the case in 1914–18, and defensive activity was therefore higher. Radar installations had started to spring up even before the declaration of war, a new technological development with strong roots in Suffolk, development having taken place at the MOD research site at Orford Ness near Aldeburgh, before moving to a new establishment at Bawdsey Manor, near Woodbridge.

Radar sites at West Beckham in Norfolk, Darsham and Bawdsey in Suffolk, and Canewdon and Great

Based on the Stanier 8F of the LMS, the War Department commissioned these powerful Austerity 2-8-0 locomotives for heavy freight. One of these, No. 7337, hauled the ill-fated train at Soham on 2 June 1944.

Bromley in Essex all employed large teams of personnel, all of whom required materials, equipment, food and transport. The same applied to the Y stations, radio listening posts for intercepting information about the Nazi war machine – these appeared at Cromer, North Walsham, Beeston Regis and Gorleston in Norfolk, and Felixstowe, Saxmundham and Southwold in Suffolk.

Even more significant in terms of their impact on the region were the airfields that sprang up all over East Anglia. War was now an aerial, as well as a ground-based or seafaring matter, and Britain was vulnerable to the air in a way that was without precedent. This threat from Europe was countered by a rash of air bases that took advantage not only of the geography of the region but also its topography – the largely flat areas of sparsely populated, largely agricultural land could quickly be turned into airfields – and indeed were, the remains of which are frequently still to be found all over the Suffolk and Norfolk countryside.

Sixty-eight new airfields were built throughout Norfolk and Suffolk, a massive construction project, the hundreds of tons of material required all having to travel across the railway network, not to mention the personnel that went with the airfields. Many of these in the later years of the war were Americans, bringing their own cultural influences that must have been startling to rural East Anglians.

The Soham Accident

On the night of 2 June 1944, a heavy goods train of forty-four wagons approached Soham station in Cambridgeshire. Hauled by one of the War Department 2-8-0 goods locomotives, it was en route from Whitemoor Yard to Ipswich in the charge of its driver, Benjamin Gimbert, and his young fireman, James Nightall. The train itself carried 400 tons of bombs and associated components.

Reaching Soham at approximately 01:45am, Gimbert was alarmed to notice that the wagon nearest the locomotive appeared to be on fire – a bluish, gas-like flame was licking around the bottom planks of the vehicle. This was a serious matter, as the leading vehicle was carrying some forty-four bombs with a total combined weight of 9 tons.

Immediately alert to the significance of the problem, Gimbert brought the train to a stand, whilst Nightall leapt down from the footplate to uncouple the blazing vehicle from the rest of the train. This done, Gimbert then drew the locomotive and leading wagon forwards to explain to the signalman at Soham his intention to haul the wagon clear of the station. Before he could do this, however, the wagon exploded.

Fireman Nightall died immediately, whilst the signalman died the following day from injuries sustained in the explosion. As well as the almost complete demolition of the signalbox and station

Recovery operations after the Soham explosion of 1944. Although the extent of the damage is considerable, it would have been much worse had it not been for the courageous actions of the engine crew.

buildings, the blast created a crater sixty-six feet in diameter and fifteen feet deep, whilst the wagon itself simply disintegrated into unidentifiable fragments. However, the remainder of the train sustained only light damage, whereas had it not been for the swift and courageous action of the engine crew the whole train, with its 400-ton payload, would have gone up, with disastrous consequences.

Driver Gimbert was seriously injured, but miraculously survived the accident, both enginemen subsequently being awarded the George Cross for their bravery, Nightall of course receiving his posthumously.

Two Class 47 locomotives were later named for the two men, both locomotives being allocated to Stratford shed, although upon withdrawal the names were transferred to Class 66 engines based, appropriately enough, at the revived Network Rail yard at Whitemoor.

The L&NER After the War

Once again the railways emerged from conflict in a rather downtrodden state. Not only had traffic been high and maintenance low, in the case of World War II, the railways had suffered far more from being vulnerable to air attack – although the ramshackle development of the British railway network proved to be unexpectedly useful during a time of war. This was because, unlike the railways of Europe, which tended to adopt a more strategic, arterial system, the chaotic web of lines in Britain meant that there was always another way round, making the system much harder to disable by aerial attack.

The L&NER, in common with the other constituents of the Big Four, were again maintained under the control of the Railway Executive Committee after the end of the war, whilst their attractive apple-green locomotives had been largely repainted in a sombre and decidedly utilitarian unlined black.

In a nutshell, the railways were worn out, in desperate need of investment, and all in all represented something of a problem to the new peacetime government. The immediate postwar election of 1945 had seen the electorate turn their back on Winston Churchill and the Conservative Party, despite Churchill's iconic role as wartime leader. This handed victory to the Labour leader Clement Attlee, supported by a populace weary of austerity and housing shortages, and concerned about employment for those returning from the armed forces. The new broom had a lot of sweeping to do, and one area in which its ideas would prove revolutionary would be that of the country's railway network.

CHAPTER 7

Nationalization

It is no exaggeration to say that when the nation's railways emerged from the shadow of World War II in 1945/6, they did so in a parlous state. Between 1939 and 1945 the railways had to meet the demands of a country at war, supplying the massively escalated needs of production as well as coping with an unusually dispersed geographic spread of industry that was necessary to protect the military supply lines, along the principle of 'not putting all your eggs in one basket'. And they did this not only with severe restrictions on materials, manpower and maintenance as regards the permanent way, locomotives and stock, but also in conditions of blackout, severe bombing and the continuing needs of passenger traffic, which still needed to be met – not to mention the demands of continuous, nationwide troop movement.

Furthermore, although each member of the 'Big Four' had their own locomotive works, and had developed their own types of reasonably modern freight and passenger locomotives during the 1930s, the railway network as a whole still had a huge volume of increasingly antiquated equipment, generally inherited from the old pre-Grouping companies, a surprising amount of it dating back to the nineteenth century. However, old, inefficient, worn and dirty though they most certainly were, they nonetheless continued to do sterling service throughout the war

years – though now, in postwar Britain, the whole network had started to look decidedly shabby.

These problems included a chronic backlog of maintenance, a six-year hiatus of investment and development, and mounting operating costs, and as with previous episodes in this history, the answer seemed to be further unification. To the postwar Labour government, who had won a landslide victory in the election of 1945, this meant nationalization.

To Attlee and his party, nationalization was the answer to many of the country's ills. The years 1946 to 1949 saw the nationalization of much of Britain's heavy industry, as well as the creation of the National Health Service – and of course in 1946, the nationalization of the railways, creating the new transport behemoth that was British Railways. This was to be a completely unified organization stretching across the entirety of Great Britain, split into five operating regions broadly reflecting (and indeed, retaining much of the flavour of) the four pre-Grouping companies, the fifth region representing central (that is, London-based) operations. These sections were named, prosaically, the Eastern, Western, Northern and Southern regions, generally being identified by the initial in brackets, so this modern successor to the old Great Eastern and London & North Eastern Railways became known by the rather brief and efficient appellation BR (E).

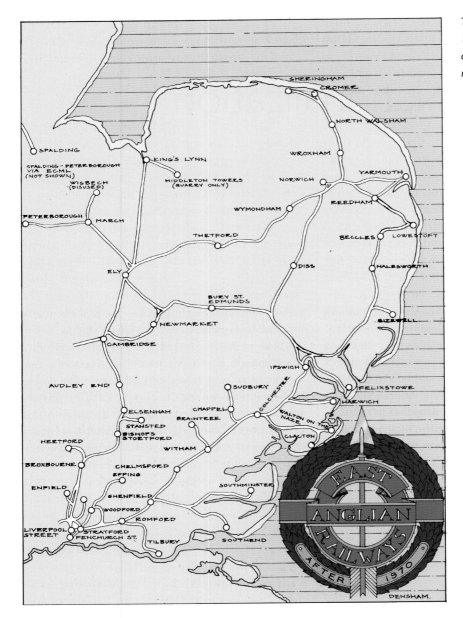

The railways of East Anglia c. 1970. Many route miles were cut from the network after nationalization.

However, the administrative shape of the new railway looked rather similar to that which had preceded it, the most notable difference being that the railways now answered to the Treasury rather than to shareholders. Each of the regions possessed its own general manager, backed by a board – in this case, a regional board, with a remit to direct and advise only, overall policy being now of course dictated by government.

The sweep of nationalization was broad and far-reaching, meaning that at last the most obscure black sheep of the railway network were drawn into the fold. Even moribund oddities, such as the defunct (since 1945) Corris Railway in West Wales, were nationalized, saddling the new British Railways with a curious 'burdensome estate' of secondhand odds and ends to dispose of. Significantly, the Corris' nearby neighbour,

An extremely weatherbeaten GER class F48 (LNER Class J17) approaches Barnwell Junction in Cambridgeshire.

the Tallyllyn Railway, which had an operating strategy that was best described as 'not quite dead', was missed from the exhaustive list of nationalized companies, with ultimately far-reaching consequences for the preservation movement that were undreamed of in 1946.

Of greater significance for the eastern regions, nationalization finally domesticated the Mid Suffolk Railway, whose continued (albeit rather nominal) independence since its opening in 1904 was nothing short of miraculous, and which will be discussed in a later chapter. In similar fashion, the rather ambiguous identity of the old M&GNJR, which had retained more than a trace of its old independence under the L&NER, was also merged into the fabric of BR. Furthermore, the directors of British Railways – directors who, for the first time in railway history, did not have a nervous eye on the shareholder, but rather on the taxpayer – were now obliged to start totting up the figures – and by now, it should evince no surprise that the figures did not look good.

Haughley Junction – change for MSLR. Struggling lines meant the Mid-Suffolk had little chance of survival in the new nationalized network.

A Doubtful Bargain

The nation had bought the railways, lock, stock and barrel from a smorgasbord of private shareholders. The sums involved in the transfer of the railways from private to public enterprise were unprecedented in the annals of public service – and it was a dubious asset that had been acquired. The British government had paid full price for a theoretically functional railway network that was in truth worn out and exhausted, with a six-year backlog of maintenance as a result of the war, and a desperate need for modernization, rationalization and investment. This meant that in effect, BR was saddled with debt before it had even started, whilst the huge national pressure on manufacturing to feed the export trade meant that the demands placed on freight traffic remained high.

Passengers no longer needed to consider whether their journey was 'really necessary', as had been demanded of them during the war years, and given the developing weariness with austerity amongst the general public, would no doubt have been reluctant to do so if asked. Those who had been away fighting were returning in their droves, eager for a standard of living higher than the one they had left behind, and for full employment – and for a country pursuing a policy of production at a high volume, there was plenty of employment available. For most people cars were still an unachievable luxury, and petrol was still scarce – so the railways still had a significant role to play in providing transport for the masses.

The Postwar Railway

One of the major problems facing the railways was the need for an immediate solution to a severe motive power crisis – which, just to complicate matters, was effectively two crises rolled into one largely

An interior view of Stratford Works in the early 1950s.

unmanageable package. In short, there was a paucity of reliable, up-to-date locomotive power, since the non-standardized, ageing collection of pre-Grouping locomotives was ill-suited to this new era of nationalization.

Coupled to this was a recognized need for modernization – the prewar railways had been experimenting with new forms of locomotion, most notably the LMS with their prototype diesel-electric locomotives, but the L&NER had also experimented with diesel-electric traction in 1935, and developed the successful Class AM6 EMU for the Liverpool Street–Shenfield route in 1938. These new forms would ultimately break the monopoly that steam had held across the British railway network for over a hundred years, and this was unarguably the direction that the postwar railway would have to take.

But to revolutionize rail traction would take time, and a period of experimentation, crystallizing in the 'Modernization Plan' of 1956, not now universally regarded as a success. However, that didn't deal with the immediate crisis, which could only be solved quickly by exploiting existing techniques and knowledge – and *that* meant building just shy of a thousand brand-new steam locomotives, to standardized patterns.

Excellently designed they undoubtedly were, but they were conceived, designed and built in the full knowledge that steam was by now seen as a blind alley, and that they would be obsolete before they had completed half of the normal projected lifespan of

British Railways' standard locomotive designs were mostly doomed to have a short working life. Looking remarkably clean, No. 80092 was one of many 4MT tank locomotives built. It was scrapped in 1966.

a steam locomotive. The distillation of this inevitable and largely unavoidable folly acquired physical heft in the form of No. 92220 *Evening Star*, a BR standard 9F freight locomotive, 86 tons in working order, and the 999th – and the last – steam locomotive to be built by British Railways. She was completed in 1960, and BR let the curtain fall on steam traction in 1968. Out of this eight-year lifespan, *Evening Star* saw only five years in service before being withdrawn and ultimately sold into preservation.

To put this into context, one could take the extreme opposite example of the doughty and numerous J15 class of locomotive familiar on light passenger and freight duties all over East Anglia.

Examples of the type were stationed at Yarmouth, Colchester, Lowestoft, Ipswich and Norwich, and were regularly seen on branch-line service up until 1962, when the last few were finally withdrawn. The design first appeared on the GER in 1883, giving the oldest of these locomotives a service life of almost eighty years. In fact one example, GER No. 564 (BR No. 65462), remains at work on the North Norfolk Railway to this day.

A significant impact of the introduction of the new standard locomotive types was the appearance in East Anglia of the unromantically named BR Standard Class 7, otherwise known as the Britannia class after No. 70000, the first of the series. These 4-6-2

The workhorses of East Anglia. J15 No. 65477 is seen here at Cambridge, bearing the D31 Cambridge shed number. An unidentified sister locomotive sits behind. Grubby and unkempt, these old stagers nonetheless carried on their work until the early 1960s.

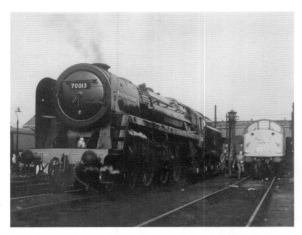

Seen here on the last day of BR steam at Lostock Hall Shed, Preston in 1968, No. 70013 Oliver Cromwell *is about to begin a new life in preservation at Bressingham in Norfolk.*

'Pacific' mixed traffic locomotives, like most of the standard designs, had more than a whiff of the LMS about them in appearance, perhaps unsurprisingly as they had been constructed at the old Midland works at Crewe, but in fact owed more to the Southern in terms of their constructional details.

Capable, on a good road, of 90mph (145km/h), popular with locomotive crews and possessed of generous reserves of power relative to their weight, the newcomers soon set about shaking up journey times across the region. Examples of the class were stabled at Norwich and Stratford to take over the Norwich–Liverpool Street services, a task that they took in their stride, achieving a journey time of just over two hours – a timing that is little different to those achieved today, the best contemporary (timetabled) time being two hours and two minutes – only eight minutes faster than the Britannias. Their presence was also felt on the London to Cambridge services, where once again the standards shaved a healthy chunk off the times set by their ex-L&NER (and in some instances, GER) predecessors.

As with the other standard types, the lives of the Class 7 locomotives were relatively short. Having appeared on the Eastern Region in 1951, they were gone by 1967, all but two of the fifty-five-strong class being unceremoniously scrapped. Cecil J. Allen claims in his book *The Great Eastern Railway* that the

Britannias saved the London–Norwich route £70,000 per annum thanks to their efficiency and superb performance, but the routine overhaul and maintenance of steam had been progressively 'wound down' by BR under the Modernization Plan (of which more below) as being costly and inefficient, meaning that these relatively new locomotives became neglected and worn within a disproportionately short time-frame.

The last of the class to haul a BR passenger service was No. 70013, *Oliver Cromwell*, on 11 August 1968, a locomotive that had spent much of its life stabled at Norwich. This was in fact an excursion from Liverpool to Carlisle, and the end of steam haulage for British Railways. It wasn't quite the end for No. 70013, however, as she had been selected by the National Collection to represent her class. They had passed on her sister engine, No. 70000 *Britannia*, despite her being the first Class 7 built, because after only sixteen years, the older locomotive was considered to be in too poor a state to be preserved. (No. 70000 *was* bought, however, by a private purchaser, and survives today.)

No. 70013 effectively entered preservation as soon as her work was done, but since the National Railway Museum had not yet relocated to its current home in the roundhouse at York, they had nowhere to put their sizeable acquisition. They knew a man who did though, and thus it was that the locomotive soon found itself heading back to its old stomping ground of East Anglia (under her own power, in a rather flagrant disregard of the ban on steam that had come into effect after the 11th) and the developing museum at Bressingham; here it remained for many years, often to be seen in steam on the demonstration line-up until the mid-1980s.

The Branch Lines Committee

In 1949 the government, casting about their new railway territory with a critical eye carefully tuned for economy, formed the charmingly named Branch Lines Committee. Sadly, this was not a committee formed in favour of branch lines, but rather *against* them – the remit was to identify inefficient and

Footplate crew and staff at Laxfield. Left to right: Harold Howell, Horace Bloor, Joe Shennier (driver) and Jack Law (fireman). When the MSLR closed, these last two were transferred to King's Cross – quite a change of pace!

unremunerative lines and evaluate the options for increasing their efficiency – including, where necessary, their suitability for closure.

Sadly in East Anglia there were a number of candidates well suited to attract the attention of the committee. One of the first was the Mid-Suffolk Light Railway, 19 miles (30km) of single-track line whose history is further detailed in Chapter 9. By 1939 the traffic over the line had reduced to a mere two trains each way per day, and after falling under the gaze of the BLC, the line closed to all traffic,

passenger and freight, in 1952. In a pattern to be repeated all over the country, locals turned out in force to ride on the last train. Had they turned out in such numbers to use the train during normal operation, they might have been able to retain the line for which they held such nostalgic fondness.

Much more significant – and far less easy to justify – was the closure in 1958 of the old Midland and Great Northern Joint Railway. Matthew Engel, who spoke to the last stationmaster to serve at Melton Constable for his book, *Eleven Minutes Late*, draws a cynical

The shape of things to come – but sadly not for long. A Metropolitan–Vickers DMU at Cromer Beach station.

parallel with this date and the need for the British Transport Commission to fund a pay increase.

This loss represented a large chunk of the rail network in East Anglia, and still a busy section during the summer months. Melton Constable was a significant junction, particularly for routes to the north of the country. But nearly all of it went in what was the biggest pre-Beeching closure to befall the British railway network. As with the Somerset & Dorset Joint a few years later – which managed to survive the Branch Lines Committee of the 1950s but not the Beeching Report of the 1960s – the railway-men, still loyal to their company, muttered darkly about traffic being siphoned off to alternative routes in order to create artificially low receipts, all the better to justify the total closure planned.

Certainly a comparison between the prewar rail-way map of Norfolk and that of today shows just how much of the county was cut off. Melton Constable, a thriving junction right up to the end and a real 'railway town', has reverted to being a quiet village once more. The M&GNJR network was swiftly lifted within months of closure – perhaps some shame was felt by those who had so summarily dispatched such a friendly, noble railway.

Further casualties included the characterful Elsenham & Thaxted Light Railway – detailed in Chapter 9 – in 1952, the line between Bury St Edmunds and Thetford in 1953, and the Yarmouth–Beccles route in 1959. Some of these lines would linger on for freight traffic for a while longer, but the pruning carried out by the BLC would prove to be a mere hors d'oeuvre compared to the dramatic cutbacks that were to come.

The Modernisation Plan, 1955

The surgery of the BLC, under the aegis of the British Transport Commission, was part of a wider plan to cure the ailments of the new nationalized railway. This plan, unveiled in 1955, was built upon a report titled 'Modernisation and Re-Equipment of the British Railways', with a remit to drag Britain's railways into the twentieth century, presumably unaware of the fact that they'd already staggered through half of that

century just as they were. In a nutshell, the prongs of this attack on the condition of the railways comprised the development of new motive power (and new meant, most emphatically, *not* powered by steam); new up-to-date rolling stock; the improvement of freight capacity and handling; and judicious pruning, as we have already seen, of the less remunerative corners of the network in an attempt to whittle down the financial liability that had been acquired along with the railways.

At this point, the problem faced by BR in its motive power department was increased by the scope of the Modernisation Plan, rather than being alleviated as it should have been. The long-term goal of the plan was electrification of the network – a concept that had been considered elsewhere in the country as long ago as 1904, but not implemented – and the Eastern Region became a focus for this, building upon the work done by the L&NER on their suburban lines out of Liverpool Street in the late 1930s.

The plan provided for the purchase of 1,100 new electric locomotives, the downside of this being that in order to run them, investment in the necessary trackside infrastructure was required, which repre-sented a further cost. In fact, the network is *still* a long way from being even close to full electrification, as we shall see in Chapter 8.

The Diesels Are Coming

Having decided that electrification was the answer, the next move in the Modernisation Plan becomes a little harder to fathom. Instead of 'making do' in the meantime with the new standardized steam locomo-tives, BR proceeded to commission a quantity of new diesel-electric and diesel-hydraulic locomotives in the hope that they would provide a stop-gap between steam and electrification whilst simultaneously offering savings. This was despite the huge outlay involved for adopting a new and relatively untested technology, and the fact that standard types of steam locomotives were (in 1955) *still* being built and put into service.

Worse, whereas the steam locomotives had at least the advantage that their standardized designs were

An AC railbus at Burwell, Cambridgeshire. The railbuses were intended to reduce the running costs of underperforming lines, but were often rather too little, too late. Burwell closed to passengers in 1962.

universal across the network (and that the various depots were well equipped to maintain them), the same could not be said of the new diesels, built by a range of companies to a range of designs, differing not only in size and appearance, but also engine and transmission details.

One notable aspect of this move to an interim measure (or, as it turned out, not so interim, as it is only now, in 2021, that a serious move away from diesel power is being mooted) was the purchase by BR in 1955 of thirty-six prototype diesel multiple units, or DMUs, each comprising a two-car 'set'. This was a concept that had been toyed with by one or two of the Big Four companies before the war, most notably the Great Western Railway, but had not achieved widespread success.

For the BTC, however, these lightweight passenger units, built by Metropolitan Cammell in Birmingham, seemed to offer a solution to the problem of unprofitable rural branch lines. Of the thirty-six sets purchased, twenty-nine were allocated within East Anglia, quickly becoming a familiar sight at rural stations, particularly on the old M&GNJR – although, as we have already seen, their time there was to be short, the entirety of that once proud railway being closed only three years after the introduction of the DMUs.

Nonetheless, they proved reasonably successful, and largely did what they had set out to do – namely to reduce the costs of running such lightly used lines. They had their limitations, however, and the difficulty of pairing them with other items of rolling stock contributed to their relatively short service life. These prototype units were withdrawn between 1967 and 1969, with most examples being scrapped – not such an impressive end for vehicles whose entire *raison d'être* was ostensibly one of economy. They did, however, pave the way for the longer lived classes 101 and 102 DMUs, introduced in East Anglia in 1970, numerous examples of which remained in regular service for over twenty years, the last (based at Norwich) being withdrawn in 1996.

Electrification

As early as 1949, the electrification of the commuter lines around Liverpool Street and into Essex had been largely completed, as a continuation of the work started by the L&NER before the war. This ensured the continuation of the original plan for a 1,500 volt system, fed to the locomotives via an overhead catenary and pantograph collection. This was a conscious step away from the electrified third rail system that had prevailed on earlier electrified

Ex-GER L77 No. 69722, seen here at Bethnal Green in 1958. Its time on this route was surely growing short, as works to install overhead electrification are apparent in the background.

lines, most notably on the suburban trains of the old Southern Railway – a pioneer of main-line electrification whose extensive investment in the ultimately superseded third-rail system meant that much of the Southern region remains tied in to the unusual practice even today.

Not that it would be entirely plain sailing for the Eastern Region, either. The work to electrify the lines in East London and Essex involved the construction of numerous substations tailored to the 1,500v system, which would eventually give way to a new 25,000v system that was later to become the universal standard. Furthermore, the works also included the replacement of the old mechanical signalling systems with electric four-aspect colour light signalling and junction control, which in turn would allow train movements to be controlled not by an army of signalmen in their widely dispersed mechanical cabins, but from two gleaming new control rooms at Liverpool Street and Stratford. In London and the suburbs at least, it was beginning to look as if the modern railway might actually become a reality.

1963: The Reshaping of Britain's Railways

One of the most controversial initiatives of the postwar nationalized railway was the imposition of severe cutbacks on the route mileage of the network. This was done for reasons of economy, and whilst few would argue that economies were needed, the *modus operandi* has been the cause of much bitterness and resentment in subsequent years.

The name upon everybody's lips when one mentions the drastic pruning of the British railway network in the early 1960s is, of course, that of Dr Richard (later Baron) Beeching, the author of a much-maligned report, *The Reshaping of Britain's Railways*, published in 1963. This outlined a thorough cull of route miles across the United Kingdom, reducing the overall network by 30 per cent (a loss of approximately 5,000 miles) as well as the closure of some 2,363 stations. By definition, the bulk of these were in sparsely populated rural locations – poor prospects in terms of traffic receipts, but still of importance as far as the economic growth of those areas was concerned.

The report prepared by Beeching was an advisory, rather than stipulatory document, the need for which had been identified in 1960 by the then Prime Minister, Harold Macmillan. Macmillan wanted to see the railway network adapted to meet modern needs and conditions, a part of this being that the railways should be run *profitably*. This last must have been a remarkable piece of pie-in-the-sky thinking, it being almost unheard of for a

The surviving railway station at Snape, Suffolk. It rarely saw a conventional passenger, and mostly dealt with freight from the adjacent Maltings. It is now a private house.

Inside, many original features remain lovingly preserved and in situ as a reminder of its railway past, no doubt helped by extremely minimal footfall.

railway company, be it privately or state owned, to be run at a profit. Arguably it was this conceit that became the main flaw in the ideology of the 'Reshaping' report.

A further flaw was the report's publication during the tenure of Ernest Marples as Minister of Transport. Whatever the truth of Marples' role in the *Reshaping* programme, he was seen as something of a dodgy character. He acquitted himself well as Postmaster General between 1957 and 1959, during which time he introduced premium bonds, STD dialling codes and the British postcode system (which latter scheme was initially trialled in and around Norwich in 1959). However, his subsequent appointment as Minister of Transport earned him much criticism – perhaps justly, as he culminated his career by fleeing the country to live in Monaco, his unexpected departure oddly coinciding with the end of the 1974 tax year. Having avoided paying tax via a company in Liechtenstein for some years, his flight was ultimately unsuccessful and he was obliged to repay £7,600 to the British Treasury after his assets in the UK were frozen.

More relevant to the plan to reshape Britain's railways, however, was the scandal that surrounded Marples' failure to declare an interest in the civil engineering company Marples Ridgway, although the sharp-eyed might have deduced some level of association based on the company's name alone.

His wrists were firmly slapped for this, and he was instructed by the government to sell his 80 per cent shareholding in the company, with which he swiftly complied – by selling them to his wife.

Whilst it is by no means certain, it could be inferred that through the railway closures – and their inevitable replacement by new motorway routes, built by civil engineering companies in which Marples had a financial interest – the Minister of Transport enjoyed a rich personal harvest. Perhaps, as Macmillan had hoped, the reduction of the railway network *did* make a profit – it was just unfortunate that such profits flowed into the pockets of his minister, rather than into the public coffers of Great Britain, as presumably the Premier had hoped.

To return to Dr Beeching, it is fair to say that the man was far less unscrupulous than Marples, although arguably no less unpopular. Nowadays his name is used almost as a shorthand for the state of the

modern British railway network, or rather the lack of it; it was sufficiently universal in its recognition for it to become the title of a BBC television comedy series in 1995, starring much of the old *Hi de Hi!* cast as the staff of a rural branch-line station facing closure as an 'unremunerative' route.

But in the early 1960s, Beeching's name was reviled not so much for *what* he was doing, but what he got *paid* to do it: £24,000 per annum. This was a wage match with his former salary at ICI, and was offered in order to lure him into accepting the post of Chairman of the British Transport Commission for five years. At that time this was a staggering sum, over twice the wage of any other chairman of any nationalized industry. The papers referred to it as the 'Beeching bombshell' – although perhaps they little realized what was to come.

In fact what was to come was more or less what Beeching suggested – although in later years he expressed a wish that he'd actually pruned *more* of the network away, whilst most would contend that what he'd already done was severe enough. The exceptions tended to arise from political rather than practical considerations – for example, if a branch-line ran through a marginal seat.

One of the examples given by Beeching in his report was that of the line from Thetford to Swaffham. This little line was built in 1868 by the Thetford &Watton Railway Company and connected with the Lynn & Dereham, being taken over by the GER in 1879. Beeching's statistics showed that, for five return journeys per day, the line carried an average of only nine passengers *in total*. Revenue covered only 10 per cent of the operating costs.

At the other end of the spectrum, however, the report recommended the closure of the mainline route from Ipswich to Lowestoft – a potentially disastrous move that fortunately failed to take place, the Ipswich–Lowestoft line remaining in regular (and well subscribed) service today. Less fortunate was the link between Lowestoft and Great Yarmouth, Beeching being in general more concerned about route duplication than he was about the practicality of individuals using the system – or freight, for that matter, of which more anon.

Some closures were inexplicable in other ways as well: Matthew Engel notes that the Suffolk town of Haverhill lost its station when the decision was taken to close that section of the Stour Valley line, originally built by the Colchester, Stour Valley & Halstead Railway in 1847, then quickly absorbed into the EUR. A concerted effort was made by the people of Haverhill and the Urban District Council to retain the railway, the local authority even offering to subsidize the passenger service. But their efforts proved ineffective, and the government, adamant that the line was unprofitable and unnecessary, closed it in 1963. One year before, in 1962, the Minister of Housing had taken the decision to *triple* the population of Haverhill, but no one had thought to take this into account when evaluating the future usefulness of the railway.

To add further insult to injury, the same section of line has since come under scrutiny as a candidate for *re*-opening – under the auspices of an

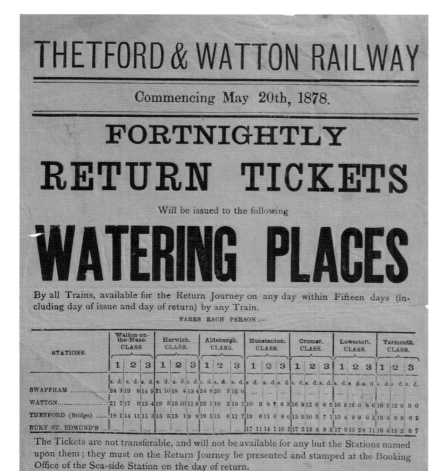

A Thetford & Watton Railway poster of 1878 advertising return tickets to popular 'watering places'. Whilst this sounds like the railway equivalent of a 'booze cruise', the destinations are in fact coastal towns where bathers could (decorously) take the waters.

Haverhill station in the early days. It closed in 1963, despite government plans to triple available housing in the town.

organization named Rail Haverhill. A feasibility study was commissioned in 2017 to look into the plans, driven by a need to improve public transport links between Haverhill and Cambridge – not least because further residential development is planned for Haverhill. Hindsight, as they say, is a wonderful thing.

Freight Traffic

Passenger numbers, however, were only part of the problem. Shortly after the publication of the 'Reshaping' report, Anglia Television sent a reporter to the Whitemoor Marshalling Yard in March, Cambridgeshire, as part of their *Here and Now* series. Railways were naturally a hot topic at that time, and the resulting film provided a fascinating insight into the operation of this huge yard, handling everything from coal and mineral traffic to perishable fruit and vegetables from Cambridgeshire, fresh and frozen fish from the coastline of Norfolk and Suffolk, livestock brought down from the North during the winter to grow fat on the fields of East Anglia, fertilizers and feed for agriculture, and the regular beet traffic feeding the huge sugar refinery at Wissington, as well as those at Cantley and Bury St Edmunds.

The feature interviewed the yard master, a dependable sort with an encyclopaedic knowledge of his business, and a strong understanding of the importance of the role of British Railways as a bulk freight carrier. It also featured the views of a locomotive driver, uncertain about the future of a job without steam, and a 'splitter', fresh to the role after a transfer from the engineering department. He had moved to pursue a job with better prospects, and had settled on the traffic side at Whitemoor, because, as he put it, the railways 'must serve the country as a whole… and I don't see any other transport movin'' the quantity of stuff that the railway can move, in one go.'

A sensible and logical man, who knew the railways intimately, his point was a good one, especially in the busy environment of Whitemoor Yard. Sense and logic, however, did not necessarily form the bedrock of then-current policy regarding the railways, and

from the mid-1960s, Whitemoor would see a steady decline in traffic as more and more freight was permitted to drift away to road haulage.

Beeching's vision for freight was one of long-distance containerized haulage, meaning the type of traffic handled by yards such as Whitemoor – of which many brand new examples had been built across the country during the 1955 Modernisation Plan – was allowed to slip away. As a result, the goods yard that formed an important component of almost every station of respectable size started to fade away as well, as the railways moved away from their role as common carrier and allowed sundry goods traffic to be eagerly snapped up by the road hauliers, a loss that proved to be irreversible.

After Beeching

Despite the glowing promises of the 'Reshaping' report, those who remember British Rail as it limped out of the 1960s and into the 1970s are unlikely to do so with fond memories. Somehow the dramatic pruning failed to promote the rich flowering of health that had been hoped for, and despite the abolition of steam, the nation's railways still seemed rather grubby, inefficient and boring. Roughly 4,500 miles of railway had been closed across the country during the latter years of the 1960s; East Anglia lost lines ranging in significance from the little branch from Saxmundham on the East Suffolk Line to Aldeburgh on the east coast (though a portion of this line remains between Saxmundham and Leiston, saved by the need to transport nuclear flasks from Sizewell B power station; and at the time of writing, a third power station, Sizewell C, is planned, although construction traffic will use the *roads*, rather than the railway) to the far more useful Ipswich–Yarmouth route.

Other closures throughout the region included Heybridge–Witham, Braintree–Bocking, and Brightlingsea–Wivenhoe in Essex, Cambridge–March via St Ives, Swaffham–Thetford in Norfolk, not forgetting the last remaining fragments of the M&GNJR, Melton Constable to Sheringham, Mundesley to North Walsham, and even Grimsby to Peterborough (via Spalding), which had played such a large part in bringing traffic on to the Norfolk company's metals.

This list is indicative rather than exhaustive, but the last-named line, a significant part of the region's network, is an instructive case. It was closed in 1970, a late evocation of the Doctor's recommendations, and a period that marked a dramatic change in the public's attitudes to rail closures. In brief, the public had had enough, and after 1970 any further proposed closures were quietly shelved. But more significantly, the line between Spalding and Peterborough was *re*-opened in 1971 – only nine months after its closure.

And this wasn't an isolated incident. Needham Market station, an impressive faux-Jacobean extravaganza, closed in 1967 and was also re-opened in 1971. Watlington, in Norfolk, closed the year after Needham, in 1968 – and re-opened in 1975.

The East Suffolk Line, between Ipswich and Lowestoft managed, as mentioned, to evade the Beeching axe by the skin of its teeth. Nonetheless it suffered privations, being reduced from double to single track along most of its length, and losing the extensive goods yards attached to most of its stations. In an increasingly familiar pattern that owes much to a lack of foresight in the 1960s, recent works to the line have seen sections of the doubled track put *back* to ease the restrictions that crossing trains placed on the timetable.

Bealings station, on the East Suffolk line near Woodbridge. Closed in 1956, the station nonetheless remains intact and can be seen from the train today. It is now used for commercial purposes.

Radio Electronic Token Block System

The line became an interesting proving-ground in 1985 with the installation of a new radio electronic token block, or RETB, system of signalling, controlled from a central box at Saxmundham, the approximate mid-point of the route. RETB was developed in Scotland in 1984 on the Far North line between Inverness and Thurso as a means of controlling trains with a minimal amount of lineside infrastructure, necessary due to the isolated nature of the country that the line ran through, and the adverse weather conditions common to the area that threatened traditional pole-borne wire systems.

The basis of the system was to replace the physical token of traditional block signalling and the signal-box equipment associated with it, with a conceptual 'token' facilitated through radio equipment installed in the cabs of trains, and communicating with a central control room. This was further trialled successfully between Dingwall and Kyle of Lochalsh, leading to its installation on the East Suffolk line.

Despite a further installation in Wales, the system failed to take off, and in fact the ESL remained the only application of RETB in England until its replacement in 2012. This was not due to any particular failings on the part of the system, but rather the fact that the changing face of wireless communication in the UK meant that the wavebands required to operate the system were now required for other purposes. The line is now operated by the system of track circuit block signalling, ironically a much older system that can be traced back to an invention by that great signalling pioneer W.R. Sykes as early as 1864.

Shortly after RETB had settled in on the East Suffolk line, a further development was taking place in the years leading up to 1987: this was the eventual electrification of the Norwich–Liverpool Street route, now known, in a well-deserved nod to its predecessor, as the Great Eastern Main Line. Now overhead wires were appearing above those rails that had once seen the Claud Hamiltons, and their erstwhile successors, the Britannias, set their impressive timings. Given that electrification had been promised in the Modernisation Plan as far back as 1955, this

Remaining at Bealings, this is the charming signal cabin prior to closure. The only remaining box on the East Suffolk line is Saxmundham, from which point the entire route is controlled.

was not, perhaps, particularly swift work – but there were further problems to face the GEML before the electrification of the route could be satisfactorily completed.

The 25kV System

It has been stated before that one key element of efficient operation on the railways is that of standardization, and to this end, after the electrification of the suburban lines outside Liverpool Street, BR had chosen to abandon the old pattern of 1.5kV electrification in favour of the 25kV system, which would now become the universal standard.

The principle behind this is one of power loss – a high voltage at relatively low current will suffer lower resistive losses over a wire of a given length compared to a lower-voltage, higher-current power source. The lower current will also require a wire of smaller cross-section, leading to a saving of materials, but as power is a function of both voltage and current, the final *power* delivered in each case can be the same. Thus the 25kV system came out on top as the superior option in terms of cost and efficiency.

The problem with high voltages, however, is that of keeping them away from places where they ought not to go, these including the earth, any structure connected to the earth, and members of the public. The fear was that the overhead lines on the ECMR would have to be installed in such close proximity to the restricted overhead structures that the voltage

could potentially arc across to any object connected to earth. On the basis of this concern, the decision was made to equip the route with a 6.5kV system, despite the fact that this system was incompatible with that in use elsewhere on the national network. Fortunately, work had only been carried out as far as Southend before it was realized that 25kV could, in fact, be tamed rather more effectively than had initially been supposed, and the system was brought into line in the early 1980s.

The Age of the Train

The reputation of British Rail during the 1970s was at a low ebb, and in an attempt to counter this, BR declared 1981 to be the 'Age of the Train' – a campaign that has aged particularly badly due to an unfortunate choice of celebrity endorsement, and wasn't terribly effective at the time. 'Eightyone is the Age of the Train' declared the British comedian Mike Yarwood in his skit of the TV adverts released by BR, 'and some of them are even older!'

It was of course an exaggeration, but not a huge one. Many of the trains *were* old and in need of replacement, much of the equipment dating back to the 1950s or 1960s. The electrification of the ECMR took care of that, but many smaller routes were still looking rather careworn, especially those with early DMUs and EMUs (remember, the old L&NER AM6

Ipswich in 1985. From left to right: a BR Class 101 DMU, a Class 86 electric and a Class 31 diesel locomotive. Note the overhead cables – the London–Norwich electrification was completed in 1987.

units were still in use around Shenfield until 1981, and the first examples of those were built before the war), and an update was badly needed.

Something new certainly turned up for passengers on the East Suffolk line in 1980, in the shape of the Leyland Experimental Vehicle One (LEV1), although whether this was what they had in mind is debatable. It sounded exciting, apart from the fact that it was prefaced by the name Leyland, another stock joke in Britain in the 1970s and 1980s. It was a prototype light railcar, essentially built down to a budget by bolting the superstructure of a Leyland bus on to the frames of a departmental rail wagon, and then grafting a diesel engine and mechanical transmission into the mix.

It was enterprising and cheap, but not an unqualified success – the transmission proved unreliable, as did the electrics, the vehicle frequently failed to trigger track circuits, goods wagon suspension somehow gave a bumpier ride than was acceptable for passenger stock, they were noisy, and the seats were narrow and uncomfortable (they were, of

course, designed for a bus). British Rail promptly ordered a fleet of units built to the same pattern, but fortunately for the Eastern Region sent them all north, where they were meant to provide a twenty-year stopgap. Many of them remained in service until 2020, and some in Wales are still in service.

The guinea-pigs on the East Suffolk line did get their new trains however, in the form of the Class 156 Super Sprinters, which quickly became a familiar sight on rural routes. These were altogether more successful and had long and productive lives, with the unusual distinction of having their interiors designed by Tickford, Aston Martin's coachbuilding arm at the time.

Sadly, Aston Martin interiors alone couldn't erase the slightly grubby air of BR, and although the Inter-City High Speed Trains did rather better on the main-line routes, towards the end of the 1980s the standing joke was proving difficult to shift. There were other factors going on too, which suggested that the era of the nationalized industry might be drawing to a close.

CHAPTER 8

The Modern-Day Railway in East Anglia

The railway network across East Anglia grew, almost like Topsy, from the now long-forgotten efforts of companies such as the Eastern Counties and the Eastern Union; it was graced by such proud organizations as the Great Eastern and the Midland & Great Northern Joint, unified and streamlined by the London & North Eastern Railway during the 1920s and 1930s, until finally it passed, war-scarred, dirty and looking decidedly dated, into the national ownership of British Railways – only to be brutally pruned back to a supposedly efficient minimum.

Today it is owned (as are the rest of the nation's railways) by Network Rail, being part of their Anglia Region, which (by their definition, not that of the author) includes Suffolk, Norfolk, Essex, 'parts' of Cambridgeshire, Hertfordshire and 'parts of Greater London'. Effectively a 'QUANGO' (or 'quasi-autonomous government organization'), Network Rail is owned by the taxpayer, but is theoretically independent of government.

This rather peculiar halfway house in an era of otherwise privatized rail transport is largely a result of a disaster that occurred at Hatfield in Hertfordshire in 2000. On 17 October that year, a London–Leeds train operated by the franchise holder GNER left the rails at 115mph (185km/h) while travelling through Hatfield at 12:23. Whilst the leading

On 15 October 2012, Class 90 No. 90011 waits at Liverpool Street, wearing the then current blue livery of Abellio Greater Anglia.

locomotive and coach remained upright and on the rails, the following train did not, and broke into three sections, while the eighth vehicle, a dining car, overturned and struck a lineside gantry. Four people died in this vehicle, and overall some seventy passengers were injured.

The investigation into the accident found that the primary cause had been a phenomenon known as 'rolling contact fatigue' – an obscurely technical phrase that found an unwelcome currency in the limelight of public conversation during the weeks following the incident. This fatigue had caused a rail to fracture under the train as it passed. It triggered a rash of speed restrictions across the national network in fear of further incidences of the problem.

Disturbingly, it was further discovered that the problem at Hatfield had been known about by Railtrack PLC, the privatized company responsible for railway network infrastructure at the time. Replacement material had been made available for track maintenance at Hatfield, but had not been delivered to the location, whilst an internal memo in 1999 had raised the point that Railtrack's own specifications did not do enough to protect against failures of this type.

Further fuel was added to the fire in 2002 when a second accident in Hertfordshire was caused by the neglect of maintenance to a set of points south of Potter's Bar station. The 12:45 departure from King's Cross to King's Lynn via Cambridge was derailed as a result, damaging an underbridge and throwing one of the carriages on to the station platform. Seven people were killed, one a bystander, whilst seventy-six people were injured.

The investigations into the above two accidents ultimately proved the undoing of Railtrack PLC, and the responsibilities for ownership and maintenance of the railway network were taken back in hand by the UK government through the medium of Network Rail.

Privatization of the Network, 1994

Neither Hatfield nor Potters' Bar were proud moments in the new era of the privatized railway, arguably the biggest significant change to the railway network since nationalization in 1947. The divisive process of privatization was begun under the aegis of John Major's Conservative government in 1993 – the sale of the railways having been something of a bridge too far for his predecessor, Margaret Thatcher, even though she had already disposed of elements such as Sealink, BR's associated ferry service, along with the internal catering, hotel and engineering wings of the British Railways Board.

An immaculate 'Gronk' in GER livery with BR crest at Ipswich in 1994. There were usually a couple of these Class 08 shunters present at Ipswich prior to the closure of many of the yards around the station. D3760 was based at Colchester TMD, as evidenced by the neat copperplate inscription.

Privatization was based on the durable but perhaps questionable idea that money could be made for the private investor through the process of operating railways – a concept that seems to have been remarkably resilient in the face of experience. Major's ideal, as he revealed later in life, was a sort of reincarnation of the old Big Four companies, whereas the reality of the privatized railway ended up being somewhat more complicated. It was to be what was termed an 'open access' railway, upon which anyone, in theory, with sufficient financial backing and (one hopes) the requisite experience could run rail transport services.

This was, in truth, an idea easily as old as that of being able to make money from railways, as the Stockton and Darlington Railway (the world's first locomotive-hauled railway, which had opened in 1825) had initially been envisaged as working on similar principles, the route being made available to independent operators on receipt of a toll, a working model borrowed from the existing inland navigation network.

The pioneer railways of England had some hazardous working practices, but this particular suggestion was too hair-raising for the line's engineer, the visionary George Stephenson. It was swiftly ruled that the railway company must, at the very least, be responsible for the timetables and motive power on the line, a model of operation that very sensibly became the standard for the next 169 years until the railways were privatized.

The modern privatized railway came into being on 1 April 1994 – presumably not a date imbued with any particular significance for its creators – under the auspices of the Railways Act of 1993. Described, perhaps fairly, as a 'complex structure', it divided British Railways up into in excess of *100 independent companies*. In the corridors of power, urgency was now the watchword, as Labour had threatened to unpick the legislation if they gained power – and the Conservative Party, uncomfortably aware that they might not win the forthcoming election in 1997, were keen to establish a structure sufficiently that it would be difficult for an incoming government to *un*-establish it again.

In order to do this, the government gave *carte blanche* to the legal teams tasked with preparing the mountains of paperwork required to enshrine privatization in statute, which appears to have been something of a free-for-all in a desperate bid to tie up the loose ends before Labour could unravel them again. Matthew Engel, for his book *Eleven Minutes Late*, interviewed a solicitor involved. He asked how much the whole legal process – and that's only the *legal* process – cost the taxpayer:

'A billion?' I suggested.
'Not an unreasonable guess.'
'Did anyone say the whole thing was completely mad?'
'All the time.'

At this point, Railtrack still remained nationalized – albeit not for much longer – but the rest of the railway network was to be split up into twenty-five franchises that were available to be operated by, well, whoever wanted to. Rolling stock would no longer belong to the operators, but to leasing companies who would then hire them out *to* the operators. Railtrack joined the fold soon after, being floated as a private company in 1996, ultimately bringing about the results we have already seen.

The New Railway Operators

In 1997 the Anglian region defined at the start of this chapter was allocated to three separate franchise holders. Anglia Railways were broadly responsible for Norfolk, Suffolk and Cambridgeshire, operating the Great Eastern Main Line from Liverpool Street to Harwich and Norwich, as well as many regional services in the area. First Great Eastern (FGE) ran stopping and commuter trains from London Liverpool Street (LST) throughout Essex, with a small excursion over the old Stour Valley Railway into Sudbury. (For modern marketing purposes, this route is now known as the Gainsborough Line, in honour of the Suffolk artist – although for a brief and regrettable period it had been known as the *Lovejoy* line, after the popular television series filmed in the locality.)

Ex-BR Class 86 at Diss in 2004, then in Anglia green and carrying the name Crown Point. These reliable and hard-working locomotives were built between 1965 and 1966 and were a familiar sight on the Norwich–Liverpool Street service. Withdrawn in 2005, No. 86235 was exported, with many of her sisters, to Bulgaria.

The author travelled regularly with FGE in the early years of the 2000s between Ipswich and Chelmsford, and can testify to the mood-dampening atmosphere of these trains and their lugubrious green and grey – and rather poorly cleaned – interiors. Of particular note were some ancient slam-door multiple units that FGE used to operate out of Colchester at that time, the modern (albeit still lugubrious) livery and upholstery failing to disguise their remarkable antiquity.

The third Anglian franchise holder was West Anglia Great Northern, who under the somewhat inelegant acronym WAGN mopped up the remainder of traffic around Essex, Cambridgeshire and Norfolk, reaching out to Cambridge, King's Lynn and Peterborough from King's Cross and to Stansted Airport from LST.

This dispersal of services across three separate franchise holders sounds a little cumbersome, and

presumably was, because in 2003 the Strategic Rail Authority decided that all services from LST should fall under the same franchise operator, which seems surprisingly logical for a decision made in connection with Britain's railways. However, not everything about the SRA was logical – under the slogan 'Britain's Railway – Properly Delivered', it more often than not struggled to deliver much of anything, having been denied the legal power necessary to do its own job. Frequently finding itself at loggerheads with the Office of the Rail Regulator, its career was not only troubled but also remarkably short, as it was abolished in 2006 after only five years. Its function – whatever that was – was then absorbed into the Office of Rail Regulation.

As a result of this disarmingly simple directive, three companies were invited to bid for the franchise. The successful bid emerged as that of the long-haul

The Class 321 EMU, seen here in the First Great Eastern livery. In the author's memory, these were gloomy and dispiriting trains, not helped by upholstery in a rather bilious green and a feeling that someone always appeared to have eaten a curry just before you embarked. The units have since been facelifted.

Seen here in 'One' branding, a Class 170 Turbostar is captured at Bury St Edmunds. The odd sense of space at that station is due to it having been the terminus of the Ipswich and Bury Railway. Note the four silos of the sugar factory in the background.

road coach company National Express, who now branded their new rail-borne wing National Express East Anglia. Under NEEA, the services run by the previous three operators were unified, leading to an ill-thought-out rebrand ('rebranding' being something of a trope on the privatized rail network) as One in 2004, leading to confusion – and the eventual omission of the rail operator's name from station announcements – as it was discovered that passengers were unable to tell if 'One' referred to the name of the operator or the time of departure.

By 2009, NEEA had run into serious difficulties regarding the operation of the East Coast Main Line from King's Cross to Edinburgh, via Peterborough. This was a franchise for which they had paid through the nose and subsequently lost heavily upon, not helped by an ongoing financial recession. It may have brought them a form of cold comfort to reflect that they were in good company here, as the franchise holder before them, GNER, had also failed to make the route pay. NEEA quickly attracted criticism for service cutbacks made in an attempt to stem the flow of losses, and ultimately defaulted on the franchise in November of the same year in an action that cost the company £72 million through forfeited bonds.

Despite this all sounding rather familiar to any dedicated student of railway history, the National Audit Office – nothing if not optimistic – reported at the time that rail privatization still 'delivered good value for money and steadily improving services'. Meanwhile the government took the East Coast Main Line back in hand and ran it themselves until a new franchise holder could be found – during which period it ran, rather tellingly, at vastly reduced losses.

Enter Abellio

A review of rail franchises followed in 2012, during which NEEA found that they had, perhaps unsurprisingly, rather lost favour with the government as far as rail operation in the Anglia region was concerned. In 2015, new bids for the franchise were submitted from National Express, now facing competition from FirstGroup as well as a joint bid between Abellio, a company owned by Nederlandse Spoorwegen, the state-owned Dutch rail operator, and another UK coach operator, Stagecoach, in a 60–40 per cent split. Stagecoach, however, dropped out of the deal, and the franchise was ultimately won by Abellio alone.

Or at least, alone for the time being. In 2017, Abellio further announced an agreement to sell 40 per cent of their share to a Japanese trading company, Mitsui & Co., and these two companies now make up the operating company of Abellio Greater Anglia, and retain the franchise (which is due for renewal in 2025) at the time of writing.

Other Anglia Region Operators

It is interesting to note that even in the twenty-first century, those cats of the railway network who traditionally walked by themselves can sometimes still retain a distinct identity within the shifting sands of the privatized railway. A case in point is the old London, Tilbury and Southend, whose independence seemed to have come to an end under the umbrella of nationalization, but which in the privatized era has emerged as the territory of C2C, a small operator currently owned by the Italian company Trenitalia.

C2C, which started out life as LTS Rail (London, Tilbury and Southend) and has passed through three different ownerships over the years, has actually held the franchise for services out of Fenchurch Street over LT&SR metals since privatization in 1996, giving it a small but surprisingly consistent empire of only twenty-five stations. However, a small number of its weekend trains are permitted into Liverpool Street to accommodate traffic for the Westfield shopping centre that now looms over Stratford station, an interesting inversion of the arrangement offered by the LT&SR to the EUR so many years ago.

Other operators appear on East Anglian metals as well, despite not holding a regional franchise as such. Cross Country, owned by Arriva Trains, is an operator that seems to specialize in the slightly odd, being notable not only for not operating any stations of its own, but also for not running into *any* of the London termini, its speciality being, as its name suggests, the operation of cross-country services. It does, however, run trains into Peterborough and Cambridge (from Birmingham) and to Stansted Airport via Audley End, giving the opportunity if one so wished to catch a CC train from Birmingham to Stansted simply to fly straight back again. Perhaps surprisingly, given some of the controversies over railway price hikes in recent years, CC can in fact get you from one to the other more cheaply than a flight, albeit over a rather longer period of time.

Another stranger at the gates of the Anglia Region is East Midlands Railway, although this is not quite as odd as it may seem, since the operator is in fact also owned by Abellio, as the recipient of their successful bid (in 2018) for the East Midlands

franchise. Their trains cross the border into East Anglia in Cambridgeshire, travelling through Peterborough and Ely and onwards to Thetford in Norfolk, just as the trains of the old Great Northern Railway used to do before the Grouping. In fact, the trains of the *new* Great Northern do it too, the latter being the franchise holder for routes travelling north and south of the capital, as well as some along the south coast, this latter compelling them to operate trains both on the 25kV overhead electric system and the legacy third-rail 750v system developed by the Southern Railway. Their East Anglian foray, however, brings their trains into King's Lynn via Cambridge and Ely.

New Rolling Stock

As part of their commitment to the current franchise, Abellio have notably instigated a programme of improvements across the Anglia region, the most significant of which has to be the introduction of new rolling stock on major routes to replace the gracefully ageing InterCity stock that had been inherited from NEEA. These last had been progressively refurbished during the earlier part of Abellio's tenure, but 2020 saw the introduction of new fleets of both Class 745 electric multiple units (known, incongruously, as FLIRTs – or *Flinker Leichter Intercity und Regional-Triebzug* – built by Stadler, in Switzerland) and the Class 720 or *Aventra*, slightly more prosaically built by Bombardier in Derby, at the Litchurch Lane works that had once been the carriage and wagon works

Vorsprung durch Technik: one of the new Swiss-built Class 745 FLIRTs is seen here at Harlow.

of the old Midland Railway, although Bombardier themselves have their headquarters in Berlin.

These new trains, Greater Anglia claimed, would 'transform rail travel', touting them as being both faster and more efficient, as well as offering increased seating capacity over the old stock they replaced. Furthermore, they would incorporate that holy trinity of the technological age: plug sockets, USB charging points and Wi-Fi, as well as improved accessibility compared to the older trains, with a lowered loading floor and retractable steps to ensure that no longer will passengers be required to 'mind the gap', or *Achte auf die lücke*, if you prefer. In an article for *Rail Business Daily* on 29 July 2020, the operating company quoted an improvement in punctuality to as much as 99 per cent on those routes using the Stadler-built trains, although perhaps to put this into perspective, it should be borne in mind that passenger traffic levels were at an all-time low in July of that year, due to international events far beyond the control of Greater Anglia.

Not that there weren't problems with the new trains when they were introduced into service. Issues with the on-board software and its communication with the signalling systems already in use were quoted as holding up services, whilst some rather embarrassing incidents – notably an automatic pantograph failing in its ability to be sufficiently automatic and

consequently striking an overbridge at Elmswell, and a near miss with a car at Thorpe End level crossing in Norfolk due to the new stock failing to trigger an automatic crossing barrier – rather took the gloss off the new trains in the eyes of the travelling public. The fact that the old stock had been 'cascaded' down on to other parts of the network with rather indecent haste meant that Greater Anglia was committed to the new trains, the resultant service delays being another point of criticism for the general public.

Investigations were made into the early failures of the new stock, which included testing components of the signalling systems used, and the interaction between them and the on-board technology of the trains, as well as – rather splendidly – the effects upon the systems caused by fallen leaves on the line. Reginald Iolanthe Perrin may be gone from our screens, but it appears that on the Anglia Region at least, he is in no way forgotten.

Proposed Improvements in the Anglia Region

The new rolling stock represents examples of what are termed 'bi-mode' trains, meaning they are equipped to operate using their own internal power as well as deriving traction current from a remote source via the overhead electrification network (at least, when

Once a familiar sight for travellers on the East Suffolk line, Super Sprinter No. 156422 waits in the bay platform at Ipswich. These old stalwarts were finally withdrawn in 2020 to commence new lives in the West Midlands.

the pantographs operate correctly). The continued need for stock of this pattern is due to the fact that within the Anglia Region, only the London–Norwich route is currently electrified (and the suburban routes around Liverpool Street). It would be interesting to reflect on how differently things might have turned out had the Modernisation Plan in the 1950s not invested quite so heavily in diesel traction at a time when that investment could have been ploughed into electrification of the network, with a longer term benefit overall.

Nonetheless, whilst the concept of electrification might have been sleeping, it is certainly not dead. In the new era of sustainability and energy consciousness, plans are afoot to increase the scope of electrification within the Anglia Region. On 13 October 2020, the *East Anglian Daily Times* announced that Network Rail, in response to a government proposal to rid the country of diesel locomotives within twenty years, had unveiled plans to electrify the Haughley–Peterborough section and the branch into Felixstowe, to allow electric traction to handle the heavy containerized freight over that route. This, it is suggested, should be implemented by 2040.

Further electrification of other routes within the region – such as that between Ipswich and Cambridge, until recently the stomping ground of the rather elderly but durable Class 156 Super Sprinters (now replaced by the new Stadler Class 755s) – is projected to take place around 2050 – or to put it another way, ninety-five years since the recommendation of total electrification was made in the Modernisation Plan (and 146 years since the Lancashire & Yorkshire Railway pioneered main-line electrification on their Liverpool–Southport line). Other candidates for electrification under this longer timescale include Newmarket–Cambridge, Norwich–Ely, and the 'Gainsborough Line' – the branch line between Marks Tey and Sudbury.

Not included on the list is the poor old East Suffolk Line, although there is a suggestion afoot that this might receive 'non-polluting' hydrogen-powered trains at some point in the (presumably fairly) distant future. The catch here is, of course, that, whilst the trains themselves might be 'non-polluting', the

Even the modern railway can be atmospheric. The Norwich–Cambridge train, comprising a Class 170 DMU, is seen at Ely in November 2012.

hydrogen itself is not, as energy input is required to separate the hydrogen in the first place. This is rather in the way that electric trains only transfer their energy creation to a remote source, rather more efficient by virtue of its size, but hampered in its pursuit of efficiency by the losses involved in transmitting power over long distances.

The positive here, however, is the increasing emphasis on the railways in the pursuit of sustainable transport. The *EADT* article quotes Network Rail's hope that railways will 'rise to the climate change challenge and...maintain their position as a critical and environmentally friendly mode of transport.' The railways are, of course, in an ideal position, in that rail transport – as explained elsewhere in this book – is an extremely efficient way of using energy to move goods around – which takes us right back to the horse tramways of Essex in 1803. Whether the Anglia Region will emerge as a reinvented, thoroughly *modern* railway in 2050 remains to be seen, although if the narrative of this history thus far is anything to go by, the truth might not be quite as simple as that.

Freight Operations

Despite the fact that the whole *raison d'être* behind the early development of the railways was the transportation of freight, the emphasis of the modern railway across Britain is on passenger movement,

Containerized freight from Felixstowe makes up a significant chunk of modern freight traffic in the region. This is Haughley Junction, where once the infrequent trains of the Mid-Suffolk made contact with the rest of the world.

a point underlined by the marketing and brand management that characterizes the privatized era. East Anglia is no different in this regard, although even here freight is still present on the network, albeit in a much modified form that owes its roots to the Beeching era.

The bulk of freight traffic in the Anglia Region is represented by the trains of shipping containers, known in the industry as 'intermodal' freight (which in essence means the need to tranship individual consignments from one mode of transport to another is eliminated), that carry goods to and from the port of Felixstowe. This is very much a 'through' service, the trains carrying on through east Anglia en route to the Midlands and the north of England via Peterborough – once again underlining the legacy of Hudson's visionary (if controversial) ambition for the railways under his care, of which the eastern counties formed such a crucial component.

Currently the Felixstowe branch carries up to forty-seven trains a day, the seemingly endless parades of container wagons being a familiar sight to commuters as they pass slowly through Ipswich station. This intensity of service is likely to be subject to further increases in the future, as calls are being made for significant improvements and expansion of track capacity at locations such as Haughley in order to increase the volume of freight that can be carried from Felixstowe. By so doing

this would reduce the amount of traffic carried by the region's roads – an interesting shift away from the attitudes of the 1960s, which appeared to regard freight – with perhaps partial, but not complete justification – as something of a costly nuisance that the railways would do much better without. Further improvements are promised – as described above – when the Felixstowe route finally becomes electrified, making it possible to relieve the dependence on diesel haulage.

Even in the largely non-industrialized region of East Anglia, there are some localized exceptions to the dominion of container transport. One such stalwart is the occasional passage of nuclear flasks along the old Aldeburgh branch of the East Suffolk line from the nuclear power station on the coast at Sizewell, this being the only reason the branch still exists, albeit in somewhat truncated form. These run via London and Crewe to Sellafield, and comprise two locomotives (double heading is standard practice for this traffic, to eliminate the risk of stoppages through locomotive failure) and a single wagon carrying a single flask.

These trains are operated by Direct Rail Services, a company formed in 1994 by British Nuclear Fuels for the express purpose of moving these sensitive materials around the country, although DRS have now spread out into other freight operations. For these purposes they maintain a fleet of ex-BR locomotives, some of them charmingly outmoded – including Class 37s from the early 1960s that have been known to appear at the head of passenger services in the region when the franchise holders have suffered a shortage of motive power. Thus it has been possible in recent years to travel between Yarmouth and Lowestoft behind a Class 37.

Other unusual operations include the regular transhipment of gas condensate – known in the gas industry as 'condy' – from a processing plant in North Walsham in Norfolk, fed via a pipeline from the Bacton offshore gas terminal (built in 1968), positioned off the north Norfolk coast. This condensate, a by-product of the extraction of natural gas, is then transported by rail to Harwich, where a refinery further separates the condensate into useful hydrocarbons, such as propane and butane, as well as substances such as naptha and benzene.

Another major rail-borne operation based in Norfolk is the carriage of silica sand for the glass-making industry from the Middleton Towers quarry near King's Lynn. As was the case with the Sizewell branch, Middleton Towers lost its station in 1968,

and would have lost the line as well had it not been for the output of the quarry, which now makes up the only traffic on the branch, originally built in 1846 by the Lynn and Dereham Railway. Carried in strings of hopper wagons, the sand trains feed glass manufacturers in Goole, Barnsley and Doncaster. Due to the nature of the line's traffic, it is no longer signalled, but rather charmingly is still dependent on the exchange of a traditional block staff, in a procedure unchanged from the earliest days of the L&DR.

This operation, and indeed all the freight movements currently active in the Anglia Region, are the province of Freightliner Group, technically a company formed in 1995 as part of the rail privatization programme, but in fact possessed of a rather longer history dating back as far as 1968, if one counts the various iterations, both private and public, that it went through between those two points in time. Freightliner is now the largest rail freight operator in the United Kindom, but as with so many elements of the modern British railway, has interests elsewhere as well, being responsible for operations in Poland, Germany, Australia and even in the Middle East.

Middleton Towers station on the old Lynn & Dereham Railway closed to passenger traffic in 1968, but the line has remained open for sand trains from the nearby quarry.

Cambridge Guided Busway

Buses might seem alien to the issue in a book about railways, but the instance of the Cambridge guided busway, opened in 2011, bears particular significance, as it follows the route of the old Cambridge–St Ives branch, opened in 1847 by the Wisbech, St Ives & Cambridge Junction Railway (closed in 1992 after a slow decline that saw passenger services withdrawn in 1970), and a section of the old Cambridge–Bedford railway (opened in 1862, and eventually becoming an element of the 'Varsity line' between Oxford and Cambridge, but closed to passenger traffic in 1968).

The guided busway is a hybrid concept, upon which modified buses may be driven without any directional input from the driver, although the vehicles may also be driven conventionally on the roads. Small guide wheels, pivoted on a vertical axis, permit the concrete guides – short 'walls' that border the guideway on each side – to control the position of the front wheels of the vehicle, thus guiding it along the route. Forward speed and braking are controlled conventionally by the driver, the benefits of the busway being that other traffic is removed from the buses' path, enhancing the efficiency of the service, whilst the vehicles can still leave the busway at certain points to give greater flexibility of service than would be possible with a conventional rail-based system of transport.

The downside, however, of using such a system with modified road vehicles is that the efficiency of rail, gained from the low-friction interface between the steel wheel and the steel rail, is lost when pneumatic-tyred vehicles are used, as they rely on an extremely high frictional interface to transfer the power necessary to the road and to manoeuvre safely.

Initially proposed in the 2001 Cambridge–Huntingdon Multi-Modal Study, the busway was not universally welcomed, many locally preferring the idea of reconstructing the route as a

The Cambridgeshire guided busway, a sometimes controversial infrastructure project built on the route of the old Cambridge & Huntingdon Railway.

free WiFi on board

The principle of the guided busway. The jockey wheel shown ensures that the bus wheels follow the concrete guide rail – at least, most of the time.

conventional railway. An independent review was launched in 2010, in response to which the Cambridge MP Julian Huppert described the scheme as a 'white elephant'.

Notwithstanding such opposition, construction had started in 2007 with the opening of a dedicated plant at Longstanton to produce the pre-cast concrete sections for the busway. After a construction process that took longer than initially anticipated, the busway opened in 2011, becoming the longest such route in the world. At the time of writing, extensions of the busway are being contemplated to the west of the city as well as to the hospital and the park and ride at Trumpington, and the Newmarket Road.

Note the building on the right – even the modern busway occasionally betrays its railway past.

Since its construction, the busway has suffered ten accidents, five of which were derailments of the buses, the remaining five being collisions, one with a pedestrian and the remainder being with road users at points where the busway crosses public highways. Opinions remain divided in Cambridge as regards the scheme, a reminder of the feeling in 2001 that a rebuilt railway would be preferable to a guided busway.

The Norfolk Orbital Project

An interesting current project with ramifications for both the public railway network and the many preserved lines in Norfolk is the proposed Norfolk Orbital Project, an initiative that through its very existence illuminates the lack of vision behind the wholesale closure of the M&GNJR system in 1958.

In essence, the project's aim is to create a route for regular public services to run from Sheringham to Dereham, with links to National Rail at Sheringham and Wymondham, by linking up the two significant preserved standard-gauge railways in Norfolk – the North Norfolk Railway with its end-on connection with the National Rail network at Sheringham, to Holt, and the Mid-Norfolk Railway's line from County School to Dereham by means of a connecting link between Holt and County School, passing through the M&GNJR's spiritual home at Melton Constable and giving that village a revived railway significance worthy of the village sign mentioned in Chapter 5.

The new route would complement the existing public services running east from Wymondham–Norwich and north from Norwich to Sheringham, creating the transport loop that gives the project its name.

First mooted in 2009, the Norfolk Orbital Railway promises to reopen a significant swathe of Norfolk to rail transport, having received support from the Campaign for Better Transport (a non-profit advocacy group with charitable status that campaigns for improved sustainable transport in the United Kingdom) in 2019, who gave the project a 'priority two' evaluation in their assessment for routes suitable for reconstruction. Other priority lines listed by the CFBT for East Anglia include a Cambridge–Bedford link, as well as Cambridge–Haverhill (pacé the absurd situation surrounding the closure of Haverhill in 1963 – *see* Chapter 7) and the reinstatement of the route from March to Wisbech. In all, their website lists thirty-one lower priority routes in the Anglia region stretching across all four counties as desirable candidates for reconstruction.

An impressive amount of the land necessary to complete the Orbital Railway (a comfortingly Victorian appellation) has already been purchased through the auspices of the NOR, including the trackbed formation from Holt station to the town bypass, which the completed line will run alongside, and that from Fakenham to County School at the mid-Norfolk end of the link. Land not yet acquired for the project is now subject to a restriction from North Norfolk County Council, which will prevent any development upon the land that could be detrimental to the project's aims. In 2016 the NOR was also awarded a £60,000 grant from the Heritage Lottery Fund to restore the bridges and civil engineering works along the route, and to incorporate a footpath and sources of interpretive and educational information.

With a further purchase of land at Holt on the cards, plus feasibility and traffic forecast studies that are favourable to the proposed project, the future seems bright for the NOR, particularly as the government recently (in 2019–20) announced a desire to reverse some of the closures made during the Beeching cuts. It seems safe to say that this is a space worth watching, and that there is a strong chance that Melton Constable may, in a small way, become a railway town once more. Perhaps, if successful, the modern-day rail operators will release a special Golden Gorse livery to commemorate the occasion.

CHAPTER 9

Oddities and Independents

Any description of railway development in England – even when restricted to a given area, such as is the case here – involves a complex spider-web of trails that prejudice a neat and systematic narrative. As a result, it is sometimes necessary to omit certain small concerns from the chronology, simply because their own history fits poorly into a continuous narrative, and their importance in the wider picture does not warrant the disruption that their inclusion must surely cause.

That said, it is also true that these lesser concerns often have the greater appeal, for what they lacked in size (and often efficiency), they more than amply made up for in character. Hence, this chapter is devoted to short potted histories of some of the more noteworthy examples once to be found in East Anglia, although most, sadly, are now long gone.

The Mid Suffolk Light Railway 1904–1952

The role of the struggling rural branch line in East Anglia was more than amply filled by the charming and perennially impecunious Mid Suffolk Light Railway. Opening to traffic in 1904, the Mid Suffolk (or 'Middy' as it is still affectionately known) was a frugally built and financially rather desperate line that had ideas somewhat beyond its pockets and most certainly beyond its station, in both the literal and figurative senses of the word. The end of the line was in Laxfield – not by any stretch of the imagination a commercial hub – yet the lines passed onward through the station, over the level crossing (the Mid Suffolk was plagued with level crossings) and across the countryside, until the rails terminated abruptly in the middle of a field just outside the village of Cratfield. This quaint circumstance served as a very concrete reminder of the point at which the money, and the ambitions, ran out.

It was a shame, really, as the intentions had been good. Projections for the new line started in 1899, driven by enthusiasm generated by the passing of the Light Railway Act in 1896, which permitted new lines to be built to less exacting specifications (and thus more cheaply) in the hope that local enterprise could fill in those gaps on the railway map that held little commercial promise for the larger companies. Certainly, this was the goal of the putative Mid Suffolk company – their plan for 50 miles (80km) of single-track railway, enabling huge areas of sparsely populated agricultural countryside to communicate with services on the GER, should have had a significant influence on the prosperity of the areas it served.

It was hailed at the time to be the most ambitious scheme to have been submitted in the three years since the Light Railways Act was passed, and was

Issue of 11,250 Preference Shares of £10 each, bearing Interest at the rate of 4½ per Cent. per Annum.

The Lists will open on Wednesday, the 26th day of November, and close, for both Town and Country on or before Friday, the 28th day of November.

Mid-Suffolk Light Railway Company.

Incorporated by an Order under the Light Railways Act, 1896, by which the liability of Shareholders is limited to the amount of their shares.

SHARE CAPITAL - - £225,000.

Divided into 11,250 Preference Shares of £10 each and 11,250 Ordinary Shares of £10 each,

Of which over 10,000 Ordinary Shares have been allotted or agreed to be allotted.

The Company is also empowered to issue Debentures to the extent of £75,000.

ISSUE OF

11,250 Preference Shares of £10 each,

Bearing interest at the rate of 4½ per cent. per annum, contingent on the profits of each separate year,

PAYABLE AS FOLLOWS :

£1 on Application, £1 on Allotment, and the balance in calls not exceeding £2 each at intervals of not less than three months.

The Company having power under their Order will pay interest out of Capital during the period allowed for construction at the rate of £3 per cent. per annum upon the amount from time to time paid up on these Shares, in accordance with the provisions of Section 51 of the 1900 Order.

Payment in full may be made on Allotment if preferred, interest being paid at the rate of £3 per cent. per annum.

Directors.

F. S. STEVENSON, Esq., M.P., D.L., Playford Mount, near Woodbridge, and 5, Ennismore Gardens, S.W., *Chairman.*
The Right Hon. THE EARL OF STRADBROKE, Henham Hall, Wangford, Suffolk.
J. B. CHEVALLIER, Esq., J.P. Aspall Hall, Debenham, Suffolk.
F. M. REMNANT, Esq., J.P., Wenhaston Grange, Halesworth, Suffolk.
JOHN DUPUIS COBBOLD, Esq., J.P., D.L., Holy Wells, Ipswich.

Bankers.

Messrs. BARCLAY & CO., Ipswich, 54, Lombard Street, London, E.C., and Branches.
Messrs. BACON, COBBOLD & CO., Ipswich and Branches.

Engineers.

Messrs. JEYES & GODDEN, 20, Moorgate Street, London, E.C.

Solicitors.

Messrs. W. H. SMITH & SON, Gresham House, Old Broad Street, London, E.C.

Brokers.

London: Messrs. BUCKLER, NORMAN & CRISP, 11, Angel Court, E.C.
Ipswich : Mr. C. E. TEMPEST, Arcade Street ; and
Mr. ALBERT RANSON, Capital and Counties Chambers.

Auditors.

Messrs. WELTON JONES & CO., 5, Moorgate Street, London, E.C.

Secretary and Offices.

E. H. MESSEDER, 265, Gresham House, Old Broad Street, London, E.C.

Local Secretary.

T. H. BRYANT, Laxfield, Framlingham.

An exercise in optimism – the share prospectus of the Mid-Suffolk Light Railway in 1902. Intended to run from Haughley to Halesworth, the line struggled financially for almost its entire existence. Note once again the names of Chevallier and Cobbold amongst those of the directors.

welcomed by the GER, the intention being to link Haughley with Halesworth, both towns with good rail links, via a plethora of Suffolk towns and villages. Branches to Westerfield on the Lowestoft–Ipswich main line, and Needham Market on the Ipswich–Cambridge line were proposed, which would have comprehensively tied a number of important GER stations together.

Unfortunately, neither of the latter ambitions came to fruition, and of the Haughley–Halesworth route, only 19 miles (30km) of its projected 28 miles (45km) were eventually built, opening initially to freight traffic only in September 1904. The share take-up had been markedly less enthusiastic than the promoters

had hoped, and the incomplete stretch of line thus far built had been paid for by a succession of overdrafts, causing the bank to put a firm lid on the borrowing and forcing a financial crisis for the fledgling railway. The Treasury, interested in encouraging agricultural profitability, had offered to assist the MSLR with funds, on the proviso that the county council matched the amount – but the county council, no doubt already perceiving which way the wind was blowing, politely demurred.

The hope had been that running goods services would generate some much needed revenue, but the line being incomplete, traffic receipts were disappointing. To add to the humiliation, the railway was

Laxfield locomotive shed, or at least what remained of it in later years.

compelled to make use of the contractor's locomotive in order to run any services at all. They had ordered a new locomotive to be in service ready for the opening, but the manufacturers, Hudswell Clarke of Leeds, had rather prudently decided to hold on to it until they were sure that the MSLR could pay. Hudswell Clarke were a prominent manufacturer of locomotives, especially standardized types for industry, and had dealt with impecunious light railways before.

By 1905 things seemed a little brighter – the line was now carrying its fair share of freight (or perhaps more than its fair share, as the GER had been experiencing a noticeable drop in livestock haulage as a result of the MSLR's operations) and the company had even contrived to pay for most of its rolling stock, with the exception of a second locomotive, which remained unpaid for, rather justifying the trepidation previously felt by Hudswell Clarke.

This apparent success turned out to be something of an Indian summer, as a failed inspection by the Board of Trade in 1906 (necessary before passenger traffic could legally commence) was closely followed by a collapse in the company's finances. Debentures were due to be repaid, and there were no funds available to discharge the debt, resulting in bankruptcy and a receiver being appointed to manage the affairs of the company.

Brockford station, on the Mid-Suffolk Light Railway. The MSLR did not run to impressive structures.

This crisis so early on in proceedings precipitated the need to gain the necessary approvals for passenger traffic and the additional revenue it would bring, and by 1908 the Board of Trade inspector, Colonel von Donop, agreed that the MSLR could commence passenger services, albeit with some pertinent reservations on his part.

To be just to the MSLR, no passenger travelling on its trains could ever complain that the company had been profligate in its spending. The stations that were built were humble affairs, constructed lightly in timber and clad in corrugated iron, although no less charming for that. In true light railway tradition, they bore names as evocative in their way as those featured in Flanders and Swann's lament, *The Slow Train*: Gipping Siding, Brockford and Wetheringsett, Aspall and Thorndon.

However, the list of stations – fourteen in all – is trumped by the list of level crossings, which numbered an astonishing thirty in total over the 19-mile (30km) journey, including such patently rural wayleaves as Hoggars Road, Hobbies Lane, Little London Hill, and the quaintly named Cake Street. The trains themselves, although perhaps unremarkable in 1908, slipped slowly and gently into antiquity as the years passed, while bumpy wooden (and frequently secondhand) four-wheeled coaches remained a staple for many years on the MSLR long after they were obsolete elsewhere.

Nonetheless, the line staggered on independently until 1924 – even defying, for a few short years, the inevitable absorption into the LNER by the simple expedient of still being in receivership, and still being weighed down by debt – some £85,000 of it in total. It required some shrewd bargaining on the part of the LNER with the debenture holders – by now surely grateful that any of their money might be retrieved – before the debt was reduced to manageable proportions (roughly £26,000, a poor deal for the creditors), and the struggling MSLR could finally be absorbed into the LNER.

Large railway companies do not tend to be romantically minded, and it is unlikely that the LNER were particularly gleeful about this new acquisition. Scrutiny of the traffic receipts would have done little to lift their spirits, since takings, particularly for passenger traffic, were low and slipping inexorably lower. By 1945 the timetable had been reduced to two trains each way daily – an intensity of service unlikely to appeal to the directors of the new British Railways Board. They had sufficient lame ducks on their hands as it was, and they didn't need Dr Beeching to tell them so. In 1952, long before that infamous name had even been mentioned in the corridors of the Ministry of Transport, the decision was taken to close the Mid-Suffolk Light Railway, tin stations, secondhand coaches, antiquated locomotives and all.

A footplate view of J15 No. 65447. Note the high state of polish on the cab fittings – no doubt helped by the minimal traffic demands on the MSLR.

Bedecked by garlands, J15 No. 65447 is surrounded by locals at Laxfield on the last day of operations for the Mid-Suffolk Light Railway. Had they turned out in such numbers on a regular basis, the line might have remained open for a little longer.

The Kelvedon and Tollesbury Light Railway 1901–1951

The Kelvedon and Tollesbury Light Railway in Essex was an almost exact contemporary of the MSLR, having opened in the same year, 1904, and closed only a year prior to the MSLR in 1951. Initially authorized under the Light Railways Act in 1901, the line started at Kelvedon, where it made connection with the GER, then ran for nine miles through Feering, Inworth, Tiptree and Tolleshunt before terminating at Tollesbury, near Colchester.

Once again the area served was agricultural in nature, mostly being given over to fruit growing, which formed the bulk of the freight traffic, the Wilkins & Sons jam factory at Tiptree being dependent on the railway for its supply. Reputedly, during the delays prior to the construction of the line, Wilkins & Sons had added an impetus to overcoming objections by threatening to move their entire factory if the line were not built.

Passenger traffic was catered for, although in common with so many other light railways, passenger receipts never quite matched expectations,

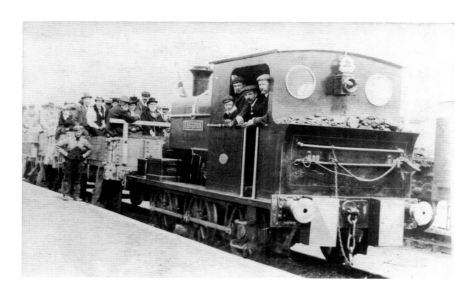

Opening day on the Kelvedon & Tollesbury Light Railway. The contractor's locomotive is seen here, at the head of a train of somewhat improvised passenger vehicles.

Waiting for the Train at Tollesbury.

A delightful period piece – those waiting to meet the train appear to have every available form of transport at their disposal, from donkey and trap to perambulators.

and the hoped-for growth in tourist traffic somehow never materialized. An extension of the line to Tollesbury Pier, the intention of which was to promote Tollesbury, incongruously, as a major yachting resort, failed to encourage the hoped-for additional traffic and soon fell into disuse; it was used to store surplus rolling stock until the wooden pier itself fell into disrepair and was ultimately abandoned.

The K&TLR was equally as frugal in its operations as its Mid Suffolk cousin, only running to the expense of elementary buildings at three of its stations. Intermediate stops had to make do with a repurposed coach body set down on the platform, while the platforms themselves were largely nominal, being built very low and requiring a step up into the train. Signals were non-existent, the railway being run on the principle of 'one engine in steam', the logic being that whatever else might happen, the locomotive should at least be incapable of colliding with itself. Level crossings were not as abundant as they were on the MSLR, but were ungated – an undoubted saving both in terms of materials and manpower, but with the cost of an enforced speed limit of 10mph (16km/h) when crossing public roads.

At its opening in 1901, the K&TLR acquired a number of coaches secondhand from the Stoke Ferry branch of the GER; coincidentally this is the branch line that communicated with the Wissington Railway, which is described later in this chapter. This illustrates well the way that secondhand stock could float around various light railways for years before being finally put out to grass (frequently, as already mentioned, as out-of-the way shelters on rural station platforms), a fact further underlined by the replacement vehicles that the railway acquired in 1929 – these were the curious low-slung continental-style coaches of the Wisbech and Upwell Tramway, rendered redundant after the cessation of that line's passenger services.

Having been built for tramway use, where access was commonly at or near ground level, they were particularly well suited for use on the Kelvedon and Tollesbury line with its minimal platform arrangements. Motive power was provided over the years by a selection of Great Eastern antiquities, mostly six-coupled J67 class tank engines. Unsurprisingly, by 1951 even the little veranda-ended coaches were empty, and passenger traffic ceased. Freight to the Tiptree factory continued until 1962, at which point the little line closed.

This later shot is interesting for a couple of reasons – not only does it show two of the ex-Wisbech & Upwell tramway coaches, but the rather grubby J69 tank engine went on to become the hard-working – and immaculate – East Side pilot at Liverpool Street station.

Elsenham and Thaxted Light Railway 1913–1953

The Elsenham and Thaxted Light Railway came about through an approach made to the GER in 1896 on the part of two local businessmen, a wines-and-spirits merchant by the name of Walter Gilbey, and George Lee, a confectioner, to construct a railway to connect Thaxted with the main line between Cambridge and London; this was not only to improve conditions for both their businesses, but also to promote the development of agriculture in the area. Thaxted, in common with many rural communities, had suffered in the agricultural depression of the late nineteenth century, and it was hoped that the proposed line would make a significant improvement to local prosperity.

Initial proposals were for a 2ft 6in narrow-gauge line, a suggestion that did not entirely appeal to the GER. Narrow-gauge lines owned and run by large railway companies always had a slightly anomalous relationship, as non-standard locomotives, stock and equipment represented a significant maintenance problem; furthermore, the incompatibility of rolling stock between the standard and narrow gauges meant that all freight had to be transhipped, a major difficulty that had been a nail in the coffin of Brunel's valiant but doomed attempt to assert the technical superiority of his beloved broad gauge. Examples existed of both pre- and post-Grouping companies owning

narrow-gauge railways: the Southern Railway had the 1ft 11½in-gauge Lynton & Barnstaple Railway, while the Great Western owned three – the Corris Railway, the Welshpool & Llanfair Railway and the Vale of Rheidol Railway – but none was without its share of inconvenience for their parent companies.

Fortunately for the Elsenham and Thaxted, wiser heads prevailed, and after many years of bargaining with the GER, the line that was finally approved was built to standard gauge under the Light Railway Act.

So long had these discussions taken that the railway was not sanctioned until 1906; it gained parliamentary approval in 1911, and finally opened to traffic in 1913.

Despite the appalling financial straits of most light railways, the E&TLR (or the 'Gin and Toffee', to give it its local nickname, derived from the trades of the two enthusiastic promoters) was in fact initially successful, with promising returns from both goods and passenger traffic. With the familiar formula of elderly coaches, J67 tank engines, and rural halts with little except a lamp and a grounded coach body, it had much in common with other products of the light railway boom, including the fact that its arrival came a little too late for it to enjoy the fruits of success for very long. Once the Great War was over, the surplus of motor vehicles returning from the Front – and the enterprising individuals who had learned to drive them – started to eat into the freight returns.

Unusually, developing bus services seem to have made little impact on the line, and passenger services continued to be healthy, although not sufficiently so to reverse a general decline in the line's fortunes. World War II brought about a brief revival, as the need to move both goods and people became paramount, but the advent of the nationalized rail network at the end of the war brought a closer scrutiny of unprofitable lines. The Elsenham and Thaxted, once so enthusiastically courted and gratefully welcomed by the local communities, now received no objections to its closure, locals being happy to lose it, providing a bus service was laid on instead. Hopefully this demand was met as passenger services were the first to go, in 1952, closely followed by total closure to all traffic in 1953. This gave the line, if nothing else, a neat total of forty years in service.

Corringham Light Railway 1901–1952

One of the odder concerns to feature in this chapter, the Corringham Light Railway connected Thames Haven, a branch station on the London, Tilbury and Southend Railway, with Corringham, a small town in Essex close to Stanford-Le-Hope. There were no stations between these two locations, the line being a short one (the total length was a mere

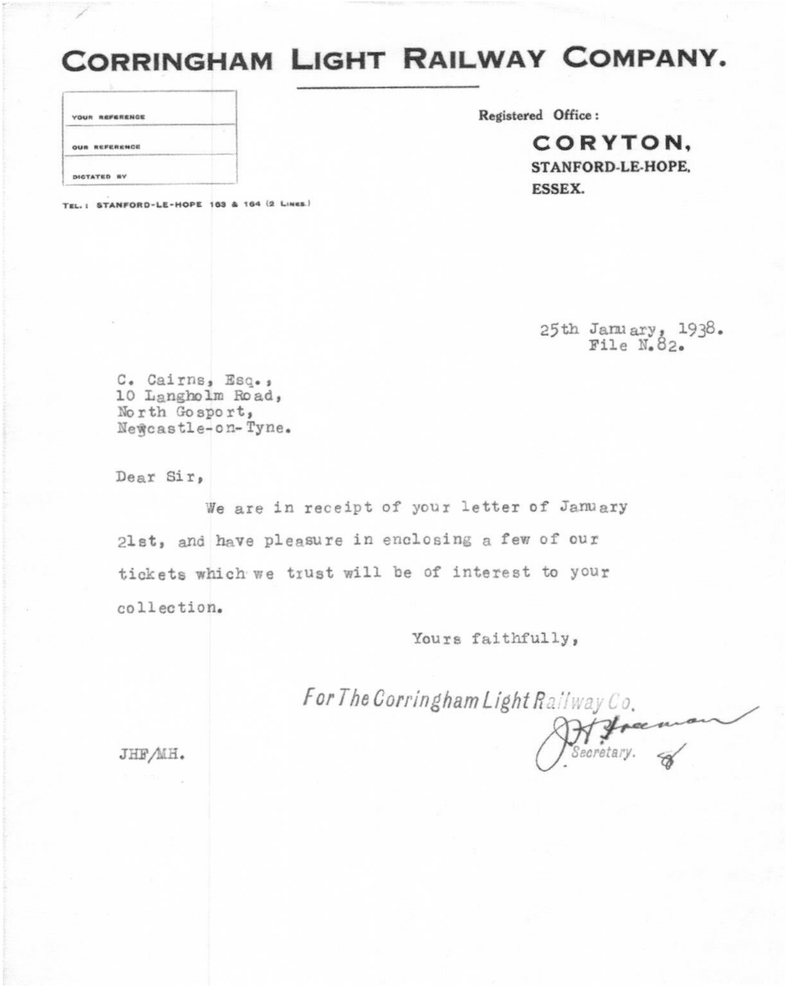

CORRINGHAM LIGHT RAILWAY COMPANY.

| YOUR REFERENCE |
| OUR REFERENCE |
| DICTATED BY |

TEL.: STANFORD-LE-HOPE 163 & 164 (2 Lines.)

Registered Office :
CORYTON,
STANFORD-LE-HOPE.
ESSEX.

25th January, 1938.
File N.82.

C. Cairns, Esq.,
10 Langholm Road,
North Gosport,
Newcastle-on-Tyne.

Dear Sir,

        We are in receipt of your letter of January
21st, and have pleasure in enclosing a few of our
tickets which we trust will be of interest to your
collection.

                Yours faithfully,

        For The Corringham Light Railway Co.

                            Secretary.

JHF/MH.

Even the smallest of lines maintained an official air, even if they could not command the most consistent typist. This letter from the tiny Corringham Light Railway in Essex illustrates how these little lines were beginning to attract the attention of the enthusiast, even in 1938.

An earlier view of the Corringham, with the peculiar Kitson locomotive. Few of these were built, the most famous being Lively Polly, *owned by the Liverpool Overhead Railway.*

3½ miles (5.5km)); but a triangular junction roughly two-thirds of the way to Corringham led to a further station at the village of Kynochtown, on the Thames estuary.

This curiously Celtic-sounding location was less romantic than its name suggested, having been built to house employees of the Kynochs explosives factory that had been developed on the rather barren site in 1895. Latterly the village was re-named Corytown, to reflect the ultimate demise of the explosives factory (through, one hopes, a decline in its fortunes, rather than any tendency to become explosive in itself) and the site's redevelopment as an oil storage depot by Cory Brothers Ltd of Cardiff in 1921. This gave the railway a further stop within the depot itself, and a captive traffic of employees commuting to and from work.

Small, cheap and in places surprisingly scenic, the CLR pottered unremarkably backwards and forwards for many years, the main traffic being freight to and from Kynoch's and latterly Cory Bros. Passenger traffic had presumably, at one time, been quite healthy, as the line owned some unusual vehicles over the years, commencing with some odd open 'toast-rack' style coaches bought new for the line in 1900. Why they were bought for a rather exposed and marshy area of Essex is hard to understand, but in 1900, such vehicles would have been seen as rather below the standards expected.

These had fallen out of use by 1915, being replaced by more conventional, albeit secondhand, vehicles

from the LT&SR, suggesting that patience had already worn thin with the bracing accommodation of the toast-racks in winter. The LT&SR coaches were followed by some of Midland origin, no doubt connected with the acquisition of the LT&SR by the Midland Company.

Locomotive stock for the CLR tended to the conventional products of industrial locomotive manufacturers, a couple of Kerr, Stuart tank locomotives being succeeded by a pair of rather smart Avonside B3 saddletanks in later years. The first locomotive purchased, however, was cut from a very different cloth, and is worthy of note – the author is aware of only three possible examples of the type, and so elusive are the necessary details that there may in fact have been only two. Built by Kitson and Co. of Leeds in 1884, as works no. T109, *Cordite* was an 0-4-0 well tank of unconventional appearance, a roly-poly locomotive that gave the impression of being home-made from discarded parts. However, this impression was disproved by the survival of a second (and far better known) example in the form of *Lively Polly*, the lone steam locomotive of the Liverpool Overhead Railway, which was used to haul maintenance trains until the 1950s.

The CLR example was evidently bought secondhand, although from where is uncertain; it was sold on again, and was finally scrapped in 1935. Various photographs exist of these engines, but it is sometimes difficult to attribute identities to them.

Cordite, *the unusual Kitson 0-4-0WT of the Corringham Light Railway.*

The mechanical arrangements closely resemble those of Kitson's small tramway locomotives, borne out by the 'T' prefix of the works number. Presumably these were built 'unclad' and fitted with a conventional cab, to fulfil such orders where a small and compact shunting locomotive was required.

Passenger traffic ceased on the CLR in 1951, and the railway was officially closed; ownership of the line (which had always remained wholly independent) passed to Mobil, the owners of the oil refinery. The portion of the line to Corringham from Corytown was lifted, but the branch to the refinery remains, still carrying traffic to the junction with the old LT&SR – so in a sense it could be said that the CLR still remains open, for freight at least.

The Wisbech and Upwell Tramway

The Wisbech and Upwell Tramway was a unique line that developed a fame far in excess of its status, linking the Norfolk village of Upwell with both the GER and the M&GNJR at Wisbech in

Cambridgeshire. It opened in 1883, with ex-Millwall Extension Railway coaches hauled by distinctive wooden-bodied steam trams, with decorous skirts to cover cylinders and motion, and cowcatchers front and rear. This fulfilled the obligations implied in its 'tramway' designation, as the line ran alongside public highways for a significant portion of its length, and prior to the passing of the Light Railway Act, constructing a tramway (legally distinct from a railway proper) was a convenient way of building a short line without it being too costly.

Surprisingly it was promoted and constructed by the Great Eastern Railway, as an experiment into using economically built lines to open up rural areas and thus link them into the national network. The initial proposal for the line had been made in 1873 through private enterprise, but had foundered for lack of capital, leaving the way clear for the GER to pick up the baton as a test bed for the concept of a light railway, using the less stringent stipulations set down in the Tramways Act of 1870 to achieve this end.

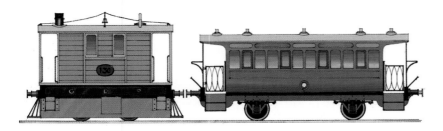

Holden-designed Y4 tram locomotive and four-wheeled coach of the Wisbech and Upwell Tramway.

The main purpose of the line was to serve the agricultural communities and bring in fruit traffic for the GER, and it became a *cause célèbre* for the Board of Trade, keen to show how beneficial such simple lines could be in rural areas. Their faith was dramatically (and perhaps, given the many branch lines that later floundered in debt, misleadingly) vindicated, as the Wisbech & Upwell opened to an unqualified success – in the early days, passenger numbers regularly reached 3,000 per week. So successful was the line that the prosperity of the Wisbech Canal, which had opened in 1795, dropped dramatically. By 1896 the navigation was no longer profitable, a state of affairs directly attributable to the new tramway.

Construction commenced in 1882, proceeding quickly enough for the route to Outwell to be inspected, passed and opened for traffic in the following year. No doubt this efficiency was largely due to the line being built by the GER, assisted by the minimal earthworks required due to the level nature of the ground it covered. By 1884 the line had been extended further into Upwell, inspiring the purchase of some new coaches built specifically for the tramway, and in their way as distinctive as the odd locomotives that pulled them.

These vehicles appeared curiously small, being set significantly lower than carriages of the typical pattern, and boasted open verandah ends with decorative iron railings, a highly unusual detail on a British railway. One of these curious coaches was later immortalized on the big screen in the Ealing comedy *The Titfield Thunderbolt*. Not to be outdone, a second example was recovered and has been recently restored and put back into service on the North Norfolk Railway, being used to represent its lost sibling during events themed around the Ealing film.

The arrival on the scene of the Outwell Bus Company, formed by a local man named Charlie Robb and taking advantage of the large numbers of secondhand omnibuses that came on to the open market after World War I, did nothing for passenger traffic. Services came to an end in 1929 with the now-redundant coaching stock being passed to the Kelvedon and Tollesbury line; however, the carriage of freight continued well into nationalization, the old GER steam trams still reigning supreme, despite a short-lived and unsuccessful experiment with Sentinel locomotives. For the last few years, however, small diesel locomotives, still equipped with the skirts and sidesheets required by the Tramways Act, replaced the aged fleet of Y-class steam trams, robbing the line of much of its individual character.

The Wissington Railway 1905–1957

Built cheaply, one might even say crudely, across a large and sparsely inhabited acreage of drained Norfolk fenland, the Wissington Railway was, unlike most of the other railways mentioned in this book, an industrial network throughout its entire existence, serving for the most part the vast sugar refinery (still there, and said to be the largest in Europe) built in 1925, thanks to the suitability of the peaty fenland soil for growing beet. Officially the railway did not carry passengers, although in truth there was a small and entirely unendorsed traffic, run rather on an 'all aboard the skylark' basis, and for a short while the railway even boasted a small coach. Presumably the Board of Trade paid scant attention to what went on in the wild uninhabited wastes of the Fens.

The railway itself was built privately, on private land, and as such possessed neither Act of Parliament nor even Light Railway status, despite communicating with the national network, and enjoying limited running rights thereon at the exchange sidings at Abbey Junction on the Downham and Stoke Ferry branch line.

The Norfolk Fens are an area of ancient marshland subject to early exercises in land reclamation, drainage for agricultural purposes having commenced in the seventeenth century. Rich in peat and little else, they had long been regarded as useless except as a source of fuel, until efforts were made to improve the land for crops. Ultimately the two most successful crops harvested from the Fens were celery and sugar-beet, with by far the greater emphasis on the latter, but prior to this growth, a valiant attempt was made to capitalize on the fenlands by extracting

Abbey station, on the Stoke Ferry branch. Not only did this station provide access for West Dereham, but it also served as the access point for beet traffic from the Wissington Railway on to the national network.

the peat and processing it to make ammonia-based fertilizers, by an enterprising if financially inastute individual named Arthur Keeble.

Keeble was a Lincolnshire man, and had bought a significant acreage of Norfolk fenland in 1904, hoping to develop and exploit its agricultural potential, to which end he experimented with a range of crops, all variously unsuccessful. What he did learn from this exercise, however, was that the fenland peat was rich in nitrogen, making it suitable for extraction and processing to produce an ammonium sulphate fertilizer, by which means he hoped to render the Fens profitable.

Keeble built a small ammonia works very close to the site still occupied by the sugar refinery today. He had solicited commercial backing to set up the industrial processes necessary for the exploitation of the peat, but collecting and transporting the raw material to the factory posed a problem on the soft and yielding ground of the Fens. To this end, he built a small railway to serve the factory, bringing the peat in and the finished product out via a connection to the GER at Abbey station. In addition, much work was carried out to drain the marshy land.

Whilst he was successful in overcoming the technical issues, the returns from the ammonia business did not reflect what Keeble, or his backers, wished to see. Keeble blamed this on the banks, claiming they had shared the details of his process with others and thus devalued his business; but the banks disagreed, the ammonia business failed, and in 1919 the factory was stripped for scrap. Throughout the rest of the life of the Wissington line, this empty ruin

heralded the approach to the sugar refinery – a case of 'so near, and yet so far', as the refinery thrived on the Fens.

Sugar-beet had first arrived as a crop in the early teens of the twentieth century, actively developed by William Towler, whose efforts to develop a fenland cash crop were markedly more successful than Keeble's. Recognizing the importance of the railway in this new endeavour, Towler formed a group of interested landowners to extend the railway in line with their plans; by 1921 he was planning the construction of the new sugar refinery, to communicate directly with the WR.

The refinery itself was completed in 1925, already some twenty years into the life of the railway, and was wholly dependent upon it, as there were no roads on the Fens. The railway was also essential for the growing agricultural community, for whom life on this rather bleak flatland must have been difficult. The village of Wissington was a product of Keeble's development, but now, in the twenty-first century, it has effectively vanished completely, the isolated houses built on unstable damp ground having long since been abandoned for more comfortable lifestyles elsewhere.

As befitted its situation, the railway 'grew like Topsy', and was subject to complex multiple ownerships; these were added to and extended by those who would benefit, and involved leases and running rights that, complex perhaps on paper, did little to disrupt the rather informal habits of the railway's operation.

Whilst 'proper' railways tended to slice as directly as possible through the landscape, the Wissington line tiptoed rather politely along field boundaries and drainage ditches, following the dividing lines almost in the manner of the Tube map – but here the sharp 90-degree changes in direction were real rather than imagined, with some eye-wateringly tight corners to be negotiated by the motley and ever-changing roster of four- and six-coupled saddletank engines.

The track itself was a mixed bag, having been initially laid with secondhand material, little importance being attached to quality or condition. Rather than run to the expense of ballast, the line was laid upon earth, although ballasting would in all probability have been a thankless task as the material sank gradually into the fen. It was a general rule on the Wissington that if the flood waters rose above rail level, all traffic stopped, as otherwise the softened ground beneath would have meant damage to this most impermanent of permanent ways.

The *modus operandi* of the WR was a masterpiece of *ad hoc* organization. Empty vehicles (mostly open wagons, and mostly the property of the GER) were dropped off at the various farms, all of which had their own sidings for loading their produce. Once loaded, the locomotive would return and take them away, leaving other empties behind. Thus they pottered around the Fens, dropping off here, picking up there, crews often collecting a cup of tea or two

en route, or 'losing' a small quantity of coal from the bunker to the benefit of the houses they passed.

The only concrete commitment in this informal timetable was meeting the freight trains at Abbey Junction, at 3:30 in the afternoon. Consignment notes were written out by the enginemen on whatever piece of paper came to hand, and the closest the railway ever came to a signalling system was the time-honoured habit of pinning a note to a gatepost at significant junctions, telling the crew on the other locomotive where they were!

Matters were, perhaps, a little more formal at the other end of the line, beyond the refinery, towards the charmingly named terminus at Poppylot. Here, the British Sugar Corporation had re-laid the track to a higher standard, and owned their own locomotives in order to marshall wagons within their growing network of sidings.

This rather *ad hoc* system of operation continued, even after the railway was taken over during World War II by the Ministry of Agriculture, recognizing the importance of the sugar-beet harvest (cane sugar, of course, had to be imported, problematic during a time of war). This seemed to be quite a happy time for the little line, with even some refurbishment carried out by a labour force of Italian POWs. After the war, the line was bought by the Ministry, but before long

An unusual colour photo of Newcastle *at Abbey on the Wissington Railway in 1965.*

Halesworth station on the 3ft narrow-gauge Southwold Railway.

it was deemed rather anomalous for the Ministry of Agriculture to be operating a railway. The suggestion was made that it should be handed over to BR, who claimed that it was *not* a railway at all – although it seems likely this was an attempt to dodge another oddball liability.

Whatever the reason, the WR was rapidly becoming rather redundant. Concrete roads started to appear in the Fens (many built by the MOA themselves), making them for the first time accessible by road vehicles, and the vehicles themselves were becoming more readily available. In 1957 the railway was sold in its entirety to the scrap merchant Thos. Ward. All that remained was the internal railway at the refinery, which took on some of the Wissington locos. By 1978 only one of these remained, albeit out of use – appropriately enough it was the Hudswell, Clarke & Co. 0-6-0ST *Wissington*, purchased new in 1938. In 1978 British Sugar decided to hand the locomotive over to the North Norfolk Railway at Sheringham. Since returned to steam, she can still be seen at work today.

The Southwold Railway 1879–1929

Perhaps the best known, and certainly the most extensively documented of the railways mentioned in this chapter, was the little Southwold Railway. A rare example of a narrow-gauge line in East Anglia, and built to the unusual gauge of 3ft, the 9-mile (14.5km)

long railway linked the popular holiday destination and fishing town of Southwold with Halesworth on the GER. Being built before the passing of the Light Railways Act, the engineer for the line, Arthur Pain, kept capital costs down by building a narrow-gauge railway under a full Act of Parliament, a seemingly sensible decision that was to have significant ramifications later on in the line's history.

Although a very lightly laid line, the SR was surprisingly neat and efficient in comparison with many similar lines. A generous yard was constructed at Southwold, the company's headquarters, with a well-built timber frame and brick station, plus a goods platform, carriage and coal sheds, as well as a shed of sufficient size to house the company's three *new* locomotives. In fact, all the stock was brand new, indicating ambitious intentions on the part of the directors – although by choosing a gauge of 3ft, they had rather boxed themselves into a corner as far as sourcing compatible secondhand equipment was concerned. This, too, was a decision that would make its impact felt as time progressed.

Travelling from Halesworth, where the SR had a modest station communicating with the GER platforms by means of a footbridge, the line had intermediate stations at Wenhaston, Blythburgh and Walberswick. This last was something of a misnomer – the station was a good mile at least from the village, and boasted little except a tiny shed, a lamp and a bench, alongside the obligatory running-in board, in sharp contrast to the other stations on the line with their attractive brick station buildings.

From Walberswick it was but a short journey into Southwold, taking in the two major works of the line – an impressive swing bridge over the River Blyth, and a cutting of not inconsiderable dimensions. Signalling was minimal, although the line did run to a block system, controlled on the staff-and-ticket principle, enabling trains to be run simultaneously from either end of the line and crossing one another by means of the loop at Blythburgh station. And traffic, for the most part, was heavy enough to require it.

Not all was plain sailing for the little railway, however. Shortly after opening, it was realized that there was neither the need nor the finances for three locomotives, and so No. 1 *Southwold* was sent back to the manufacturers, who subsequently sold it on to a railway in British Colombia; here it contrived to outlive by some years the railway it had been built for.

These locomotives were a trio of identical 2-4-0 tank engines built by Sharp, Stewart and Co. of Manchester. No. 1 was, as mentioned, named *South-wold*, whilst No. 2 was named *Halesworth*. No. 3 was rather more general in her nomenclature, being named *Blyth* after the valley through which the line ran, and for some reason became rather a pet of the crews, seeing far more use than her sisters. Trains on the Southwold were invariably mixed, and an interesting variety of goods wagons would be coupled with some rather unusual verandah-ended six-wheel coaches with an extraordinary length of wheelbase.

The fortunes of the railway clearly stabilized, for it was not long before the SR purchased another locomotive from Sharp, Stewart & Co., this time an extended 2-4-2 version of the original locomotives, which took on the identity of the departed No. 1.

Despite the jibing and good-humoured mockery that was common to many rural lines, the SR was in fact a rather apple-pie operation, the locomotives, stations and track always appearing to be scrupulously maintained. Nonetheless, the directors appeared to have lukewarm feelings as regards running a railway, and in 1904 were making overtures to the GER to try to sell off the line. The GER, however, were not keen to take on this narrow-gauge oddity, and work was put in hand by the SR to convert the lineside structures to standard-gauge clearances, with a view to regauging the line; but despite this effort, the hoped-for deal did not materialize.

One of the problems with the narrow gauge was the difficulty of transhipment – goods had to be laboriously manhandled from one to the other due to the impossibility of running the standard-gauge GER wagons over the narrow-gauge SR metals. This apparently overlooked issue was a burden to the SR throughout its existence, and represented a considerable cost in both time and wages.

Southwold station.

Nothing daunted, the next scheme for the SR was to construct a small extension to Southwold harbour, where a line was built stretching along Blackshore quay. Fishing was the lifeblood of the local economy in those days, and it is hard to understand why this extension was not included in the original plan for the railway. Mooted in 1904, it took no less than ten years to finally gain the approval of the harbourmaster, the branch being completed in 1914. In anticipation of the additional traffic this would bring, a new, and far more powerful locomotive, No. 4 *Wenhaston*, was purchased from Manning, Wardle of Leeds. But events overtook these good intentions, as World War I curtailed the local fishing industry dramatically, and the branch ended up seeing little use, as did the new locomotive, which was effectively laid up until late in the railway's life.

The replica Sharp, Stewart locomotive Blyth, *currently being built for the Southwold Railway Trust by North Bay Engineering.*

Still, the SR continued to do good business in both passenger and freight traffic. Southwold was a prosperous holiday destination, with a thriving local trade, some light industry including a gasworks and local electricity generating company, and a successful brewery, all of which contributed to the general traffic of the little line.

This happy state of affairs continued into the mid-1920s, when a local company began a bus service that started to eat into the passenger receipts. In 1927 the line failed to return a dividend for the first time in its history – quite a remarkable occurrence for a small independent concern – and the decision was taken to close the line. General maintenance remained at a high standard, although locomotive repairs fell behind, No. 1 being left up on blocks for a re-tyring job that would never be completed. No. 3 had been recently overhauled, but during the final year of operation in 1929, the bulk of traffic was taken over by No. 4, still effectively a new loco thanks to the lack of use since its purchase in 1914.

Attempts were made to sell off the locomotives and rolling stock prior to closure, but no buyers were found, thanks to the choice of the 3ft gauge. Thus the railway closed with everything *in situ*, and due to a vagary in the original Act of Parliament, no provision was made for disposal of the assets after closure. The line therefore entered an odd twilight age throughout the 1930s, when everything just sat and mouldered where it stood.

Part of the SRT's developing visitor attraction at Blyth Road in Southwold.

Restored coal shed at Blythburgh station, the work of the Halesworth to Southwold Narrow Gauge Railway Society.

This situation continued until 1941, when the wartime need for steel outweighed any legal niceties, and the whole line was torn up, the four little locomotives being cut up where they stood. Had the line weathered the war, it would in all likelihood have become another early preservation story like that of the Talyllyn or Ffestiniog railways – a case of so near, and yet so far.

Nonetheless the railway still has its devotees, and in 1994 a group of enthusiasts in Southwold formed the Southwold Railway Society, with an aim to preserve the memory of the unique line and pursue an ambition to reinstate some or all of the old railway. Now the Southwold Railway Trust, the organization is a registered charity with a base at

Steamworks in Blyth Road, adjacent to the route of the old line. Here they are developing a visitors' centre with a 3ft demonstration line and a growing collection of 3ft-gauge rolling stock, as well as an operating miniature railway.

At the time of writing, the completion and delivery is anticipated of a brand new replica of loco No. 3, *Blyth*, built by North Bay Engineering in Darlington. The Trust has also been able to secure half a mile of original trackbed in the village of Wenhaston. A second, more recently formed group, the Halesworth to Southwold Narrow Gauge Railway Society, has done much work at the Halesworth end of the line, preserving and interpreting remaining structures and works from the old line.

CHAPTER 10

Heritage Railways in East Anglia

The 1953 Ealing comedy, *The Titfield Thunderbolt*, was an unusual box office success. Depicting the efforts of a small community – led by a local landowner and a vicar with a serious case of railway enthusiasm – to save their local branch line and operate it themselves, a review by the British Film Institute suggested that 'some of the (film's) invention seems forced'. Although to many at the time it would have seemed downright absurd, it was not entirely without precedent.

With the closure of those parts of the national network deemed surplus to requirements came a curious increase in nostalgia on the part of the public for the more romantic parts of Britain's railways. Whether this was due to a regret that these charming outposts would be lost forever, or a sense of disconnection with the nationalized railway's uniform identity, or simply an idea whose time had come, it is difficult to say, but it led to a phenomenon that would in time grow to vast proportions: the heritage railway movement.

In 1952, Tom Rolt published *Railway Adventure*, in which he described the heroic attempts of amateurs to save the Talyllyn Railway in Wales, a narrow-gauge line so obscure that it evaded nationalization because the Ministry of Transport believed it to be defunct. In 1951 the preservationists took over, and quickly catapulted the little railway into the national

headlines – and indeed on to the silver screen as well, for it was this that had inspired Ealing Studios to release such an odd film in 1953.

The other significant effort was that of the Bluebell Railway in Sussex, a preservation group who took over the line between Sheffield Park and East Grinstead in 1960, only three years after it had been closed by BR. The Bluebell in particular showed it was possible for redundant branch lines to be purchased, operated and maintained successfully by volunteer labour, and paved the way for many similar organizations in the years to come. Naturally this included lines in East Anglia, and some of those examples form the subject of this chapter.

North Norfolk Railway

Given the route mileage lost in North Norfolk after the closure of the M&GNJR in 1958, it should not be surprising that the first preserved railway in East Anglia would be in that county. The Midland & Great Northern Joint Railways Preservation Society had been formed to save sections of the old M&GNJR, but their attempts to secure the North Walsham to Yarmouth section were unsuccessful – as were subsequent efforts between North Walsham and Aylsham, and Themelthorpe and Melton Constable. However, by 1963 it had proved possible for the

A busy day at Sheringham, with B12 No. 8572 in attendance. B12s were once a familiar sight across the region.

society to acquire three miles between Sheringham and Weybourne, and it was this stretch that would become the North Norfolk Railway.

Some track at Sheringham had already been lifted, so the first job of the preservationists was to re-lay this section in the approach to the station, although the station itself was still in use by BR until 1967, when a new station was opened, 200 metres to the east of the original, leaving the latter vacant for the NNR. Steam-hauled trains were run from the outset, but members of the public (as opposed to members of the M&GNJRPS) could not be carried until a Light Railway Order was passed in 1976; an amendment to that order in 1987 allowed the line to be extended further to Holt, giving the preserved line a total length of 5¼ miles (8.5km).

More recently, a physical connection has been re-established with the national network, via an end-on connection beyond the level crossing at Sheringham. This allows a limited opportunity for the NNR to operate beyond the confines of their own line, and enabling them to run trains into Cromer once more.

Like other 'early adopters' of the preservation movement, the North Norfolk Railway has been chosen as the location for a number of productions that require a railway setting. It was used more than once for the BBC television *Dad's Army* series, much of which was filmed in and around North Norfolk, as well as featuring prominently in *Love on a Branch Line* in 1994. This BBC series adapted John Hadfield's novel of the same name, which concerns (amongst other things) the family of the Earl of Flamborough – an elderly peer in a fictional Suffolk village who bought out the local branch line outright after its closure, largely for his own pleasure. At the opposite end of the spectrum, the line also appeared in the BBC adaptation of M.R. James' ghost story *A Warning to the Curious*, mentioned in Chapter 1.

The NNR has developed into a very successful preserved line, and has done much to recreate the atmosphere of the railways of the region with their extensive stock list, including both a Holden B12 in L&NER livery and a GER Y14 representing locomotives familiar to generations of East Anglians, as well as two Class 101 DMUs that worked

A picturesque view on the North Norfolk Railway.

all over the region in the 1950s before the closure of the M&GNJR network. The stations, too, seek to evoke the flavour of the railway throughout the years, with Sheringham preserved in 1950s attire, whilst Holt represents the L&NER era of the 1930s, and Weybourne adheres firmly to its Midland & Great Northern roots in 1910.

Nene Valley Railway

Aficionados of James Bond may know the Nene Valley Railway – or at any rate, they may have noticed that Cambridgeshire was not East Germany, for the NVR remains famous for the railway scenes in the 1983 film *Octopussy*. East Germany would not have been a viable shooting location for a Western film crew in 1983, but the NVR made an excellent second option, as the line specialized in European locomotives and rolling stock, a choice that has always given the line a unique flavour. The film featured a Danish State Railways locomotive and a Swedish 'B' class tank loco, plus a train comprising vehicles from France and Norway (as well as two rather more prosaically from the Midland region of British Railways). It is unlikely that any other preserved railway in Britain at the time could offer such a convincingly Continental *mise en scène*.

The history of the NVR, which occupies a 7½-mile (12km) length of trackbed originally constructed by, incongruously, the London & Birmingham Railway in 1847, starts with the purchase of the BR Standard 5MT locomotive No. 73050 in 1968 by the Rev. Richard Paten. He had purchased the locomotive outright at its scrap value, and intended to display it on a plinth outside Peterborough's Technology College. He changed his mind, however, when inspection revealed that this 'scrap' locomotive, built at Derby Works in 1954, was in fact in good working order.

It was moved instead to the sidings of the British Sugar Corporation at Fletton under the auspices of the newly formed Peterborough Locomotive Society, a group formed in 1971 to acquire and restore the BR Standard 7MT No. 70000 *Britannia*, which had been turned down by the National Collection in favour of No. 70013, *Oliver Cromwell*. Having also acquired

the 0-6-0ST Hunslet *Jacks Green* from the nearby Nassington Ironstone Quarries (sister locomotive *Ring Haw* would go on to provide motive power on the North Norfolk Railway for many years), the society were accumulating locomotives, and needed somewhere to put them.

In this the society were helped by the Peterborough Development Corporation, who in 1974 bought 5½ miles (9km) of the line, which while closed to passenger services in 1966 had maintained a freight service until 1972. This gave the PRS a railway upon which to operate, but a shortage of stock – until a request came to store a Swedish Railways locomotive, privately owned by a PRS member. It quickly became apparent that only relatively minor alterations to the line would be necessary to accommodate the wider loading gauge of European stock, and such stock was more readily available in 1974 than the British outline stock the PRS had originally planned to use. Thus the unique Continental flavour of the NVR was born almost by accident.

The line was extended further in the 1980s to a 7-mile (11km) long route, and there are hopes to extend the line still further in the future, across the border into Northamptonshire. Currently the line includes five stops besides the terminal stations at Peterborough (Nene Valley) and Yarwell Junction.

A notable 'resident' at the NVR is the ex-British Sugar Corporation 0-6-0T *Thomas*, built by Hudswell, Clarke & Co. of Leeds in 1947. Painted in a familiar shade of blue and frequently wearing a grey visage, the locomotive is perhaps the only 'genuine' *Thomas* to be found on any preserved railway, having been named in 1971 by the Rev. W. Awdry. This title, bestowed by the man himself, enabled the NVR to defeat HiT Entertainment, then owners of the *Thomas* franchise, when the latter attempted to sue the NVR for breach of trademark restrictions.

Colne Valley Railway

The Colne Valley & Halstead Railway, built in 1863, connected Chappel & Wakes Colne (still in operation as part of the National Rail Network, as well as being home to the Chappel & Wakes Colne Railway

Ex-WD Hunslet No. 190 at the Colne Valley Railway.

Like many preserved lines, the CVR is popular for film crews and themed events. On a normal working day there are fewer Indian Army soldiers in attendance.

Museum – *see* below) to Halstead. It managed to maintain its independence throughout the reign of the GER, being finally absorbed into the LNER in the Grouping of 1921. Like many similar lines, it met its end during the 1960s, closing to passengers in 1961 and likewise to freight in 1965. The land was then sold on to a private buyer, but by 1973 was resold to the newly formed Colne Valley Railway Company and their supporting volunteer body, the Colne Valley Railway Preservation Society.

Due to the fact that the lands had been cleared in 1966, the Preservation Society had to begin again from scratch, dismantling buildings from the nearby Sible and Castle Hedingham station and reassembling them on site, along with a signal box recovered from Cressing, near Braintree, and relaying track along the 1.6 mile (2.6km) route.

The change of ownership of CVRC and subsequent expiry of the lease of the land to CVRPS meant that the society went through an uncomfortable period of uncertainty between 2015 and 2016, when it seemed possible that the land occupied by the railway would be lost to redevelopment. However, a grant from the Heritage Lottery Fund, plus support from Braintree District Council, enabled CVRPS to purchase the site and secure the future of the Colne Valley Railway.

Whilst the route is short, the CVRPS have created an attractive line, in addition to which is a $7\frac{1}{4}$in-gauge miniature railway, indoor and outdoor model railways, a woodland walk and a museum

facility, as well as a new reception and shop built in 2019. The railway is home to a roster of eight steam locomotives, some of which are under restoration or on static display, with the bulk of the work being carried out by the ex-War Department 'Austerity' No. WD190. Five internal combustion locomotives are maintained in working order, including an unusual Lake and Elliot conversion utilizing the power unit and drivetrain of a Fordson Major tractor. Two ex-British Railways railbuses complete the locomotive stock.

Bressingham Steam Museum

Alan Bloom MBE (1906–2005) is a name well known in steam preservation circles, as well as becoming, in a splendid instance of nominative determinism, a respected horticulturalist responsible for the

No. 70013 Oliver Cromwell *being unloaded at Bressingham steam museum and gardens in August 1968.*

creation of 170 varieties of hardy perennial. In 1947 Bloom, whose father had been a market gardener in the Cambridgeshire Fens, purchased Bressingham Hall in South Norfolk, the grounds of which he began to develop into a successful nursery and gardens. By 1962, Bloom had started upon a collection of steam machinery and locomotives, leading him to merge his two interests to create the steam museum and ornamental gardens that made Bressingham for ever after synonymous with steam.

In addition to the short standard-gauge demonstration line, the museum includes three narrow-gauge lines. The Fen Railway, of 2ft gauge, is operated by two ex-Penrhyn Quarry Hunslets,

Hunslet Alan Bloom *on the Bressingham Garden Railway.*

The Bressingham museum in the late 1980s. The author seems to have gained the footplate of a 15in-gauge model of Flying Scotsman.

Gwynedd and *George Sholto*. In early years, this line was operated by another ex-quarry locomotive, *Bronllwyd*, purchased by Bloom from the Penrhyn scrap road as little more than a rusting set of frames, and subsequently restored to working order. The locomotive has more recently (2010) been sold to the Statfold Barn Railway at Tamworth.

The Waveney Valley Railway is a 15in-gauge line largely in the capable hands of two German Pacifics, *Rosenkavalier* and *Mannertreu*, built by Krupp in 1937 for a trade fair at Dusseldorf. These two machines provided sterling service from their purchase in 1973 until 2011 and 2008 respectively, when they were withdrawn for overhaul, their duties being taken over by a 2-6-2T *St Christopher* built by the Exmoor Steam Railway in 2001.

The Garden Railway, which, as the name suggests, takes a scenic route around the Bressingham Gardens, is currently the smallest gauge railway at Bressingham, having been built to a gauge of 10¼in in 1998. It is operated by a scaled-down replica Quarry Hunslet named *Alan Bloom*, built specifically for the garden line at the time of its construction.

The standard-gauge collection contains a wide and interesting range of locomotives, from the diminutive 1896 Neilson saddletank built for the restricted clearances on the Beckton gasworks system, to the mammoth Beyer-Garratt articulated locomotive *William Francis*, ex-Baddesley Quarry and the only surviving standard-gauge Garratt locomotive in Great Britain. However, the nature of the museum at Bressingham is such that most of the standard-gauge locomotives are on static display, with only one, LBSCR A1 *Martello* holding a current boiler certificate at the time of writing.

As well as the railways and locomotive sheds, the museum maintains a collection of traction engines and portable engines, many built by manufacturers in Norfolk, as well as vintage road vehicles and other artefacts. To complete the Norfolk connection, Bressingham also has a dedicated 'Dad's Army' museum, commemorating the long connection between the making of that series and the county of Norfolk.

East Anglian Railway Museum

The East Anglian Railway Museum, at Chappel and Wakes Colne station on the old Sudbury branch of the GER, owes its foundation to the Stour Valley Railway Preservation Society, who in 1968 leased the by then unused goods yard and station buildings at Chappel from British Railways to create a railway museum.

Renaming themselves the East Anglian Railway Museum in 1986, the organization has set out

The East Anglian Railway Museum. The well-preserved goods shed in the background has an unusual significance in the world of 1990s Britpop.

to preserve, document and interpret the history of railways in the region, with a focus on display being funded by a creative programme of special events. As well as two popular beer festivals, held in February and September, the museum maintains a programme of events including the ubiquitous 'Days Out with *Thomas*', World War II themed events, Steampunk days, model railway shows and theatrical performances.

One of the more unusual events perhaps hosted by any railway museum was a return concert by the 1990s Britpop band Blur in 2009, as a homage to the group's first ever concert given in the goods shed of the station back in 1988. This event is commemorated by a plaque on the station building, unveiled by the Performing Rights Society in 2009.

Wells & Walsingham Light Railway

The Wells & Walsingham Light Railway is a 4-mile (6.4km) long, 10$^1/_4$in-gauge line that plys its trade between Wells-next-the-Sea on the North Norfolk coast and the inland village of Walsingham. The village attracts pilgrimage to its shrines dedicated to the Virgin Mary, established in 1053

with the construction of the Chapel of Our Lady of Walsingham by Lady Richeldis de Faverches, who is recorded as having had a series of three visions of the Virgin Mary at that location.

The W&WLR was constructed in 1982 under a Light Railway Order (not normally the case for a miniature line), meaning that it can claim to be 'The world's smallest public railway'. The project was the brainchild of Lt Cdr Roy Francis (1922–2015), a retired naval officer who had seen service on the notorious Arctic convoys during World War II.

A lifelong railway enthusiast, Francis operated a portable miniature railway during the 1960s and 1970s, visiting fairs and other outdoor events, before setting up a more permanent attraction at Wells-next-the-Sea in 1976. This was the Wells Harbour Railway, an enterprise carried out in conjunction with Norfolk Council. A miniature line, only 1,200 yards long, it remains in operation today, although by 1980 Francis had sold the line on to concentrate on the construction of the longer line to Walsingham.

The W&WLR took advantage of the old trackbed of the Wells & Fakenham Railway of 1857. This line was absorbed as part of the GER as one of its routes into Norfolk, and by the time of nationalization had

Norfolk Hero, *the impressive 10^1/$_4$in-gauge Garrett of the Wells & Walsingham Light Railway.*

attracted the unwelcome attention of the Branch Lines Committee, passenger trains being withdrawn in 1955 in favour of diesel railcars. It struggled on into the Beeching era, but in 1964 all services were terminated and the line was closed.

Francis' attention had been drawn to the trackbed in 1979, and by 1982 the new railway opened to the public after three year's labour, including the re-excavation of a cutting that had been used in the intervening years for the dumping of waste. Services opened with the small six-coupled locomotive *Pilgrim* (in homage to the religious site at Walsingham), but it soon became apparent that locomotives would need a far greater reserve of power to cope with the gradients on the line and the volume of passengers being conveyed.

This situation led to the construction, in 1987, of the remarkable (and justly famous) No. 3 *Norfolk Hero*, an unusual 2-6-0+0-6-2 articulated steam locomotive built on the Garrett principle, the boiler and cab being slung between two power bogies, which carry fuel and water fore and aft. The new locomotive proved very successful, as well as being a unique attraction for enthusiasts in its own right, and became the mainstay of services on the W&WLR from that

point. It handled the bulk of services until 2010, when a second new-build Garratt, constructed to the same pattern, No. 6 *Norfolk Heroine*, was brought into service.

The line also owns two internal combustion-engined locomotives for reserve use, these being No. 2 *Weasel*, a shedmate of *Pilgrim* from the early days, currently modelled on a LNER Y6 tram engine, and No. 4 *Norfolk Harvester*, which has provided support to *Norfolk Hero* since 1986.

Mid-Suffolk Light Railway

It somehow seems only fitting that such a characterful line as the Mid-Suffolk Light Railway should have a museum dedicated to it, and at Brockford, near Stowmarket, that is exactly what it has. This is only a short line (although plans to extend are in progress), but it remains proud of its claim to be the only preserved standard-gauge line in Suffolk.

Another relative youngster, the first efforts to recreate some of the MSLR's character were made in 1991, with the restoration of Brockford station in true Mid-Suffolk style, and the acquisition of suitable rolling stock to recreate, as far as possible,

L&NER Y7 No. 985, seen here with a short train of immaculate four-wheelers on the Mid-Suffolk Light Railway.

the atmosphere of the original line (*see* Chapter 9 for a brief history). In this regard, the museum has restored an impressive rake of wooden-bodied four-wheel coaches, which present a unique experience for the visitor.

As well as the convincingly restored station, the MSLR possesses an excellent café as well as its own pub, located in true Mid-Suffolk fashion in a repurposed carriage body. So successful have their efforts been that in 2014 the Mid-Suffolk Light Railway was voted Suffolk Museum of the Year.

Whitwell & Reepham Railway

Whitwell and Reepham railway station in Norfolk closed to traffic in 1959: it was part of the ill-fated M&GNJR network, so was thoroughly obliterated through the auspices of the Branch Lines Committee. Opened by the Joint in 1882, it had been a station on the M&GNJR main line en route from the company's hub at Melton Constable to Norwich. Freight continued until 1964, however, as part of a long and unusually drawn-out decline; the track was finally lifted in 1985.

If the decline of the station was drawn out, then so too was its salvation. The station and buildings were sold in 2006 to a private buyer, saving it from the ignominious fate of demolition and conversion to a travellers' site that had been planned by Broadland District Council had it failed to sell. This was a narrow escape indeed, as the station buildings had already been earmarked for preservation by the North Norfolk Railway, who planned to dismantle them for reconstruction at Holt – in the event the buildings from Stalham were acquired instead.

By 2007, the station was up for sale once again, the previous purchasers' plans for an alpaca colony having failed to take off. After remaining on the market for some time, it was eventually purchased by a railway enthusiast named Mike Urry, with the intention of creating a railway museum, restoring the station to its original condition and relaying track on the site.

By 2008, work had begun in earnest, with track being laid through the station and to the goods shed, and items of rolling stock acquired by the Whitwell & Reepham Railway Preservation Society, a group of volunteers who run and maintain the museum, had begun to appear. There are now three steam locomotives resident at the museum: *Annie* and *Victory*, 0-4-0 saddletank locomotives built by Andrew Barclay & Co. of Kilmarnock, and their shedmate

Andrew Barclay saddletank Victory *at the Whitwell & Reepham Railway in Norfolk.*

Agecroft No. 3, a 0-4-0ST built by Robert Stephenson & Hawthorn Ltd of Newcastle-upon-Tyne, is currently under overhaul.

The museum also hosts the Claud Hamilton Locomotive Group, enthusiasts who are engaged on the construction of a replica 4-4-0, to be named *Phoenix*, of the 'Claud Hamilton' class of locomotive built for the GER from 1900 and named after that company's illustrious chairman, as noted in Chapter 4.

In addition the museum is home to five internal combustion locomotives, of which three – Baguely-Drewry *Georgie*, Ruston & Hornsby *Tipockity* and North British Locomotive Works *North British* – are in operational condition. It also holds a collection of both passenger and goods rolling stock, and as well as the restoration of the station buildings and goods shed, has reconstructed an M&GNJR signal box to replace one demolished in 1959. An original timber cabin on a replica brickwork structure was used, and was fully equipped with instruments and a twenty-one-lever Saxby & Farmer frame from a box in Beccles, Suffolk.

In addition to the standard-gauge exhibits, Whitwell & Reepham boasts a 7¼in-gauge railway running round the field campsite, known as the Top Field Light Railway.

Impressive as the progress of the W&RRPS undoubtedly has been since their opening to the public in 2009, Whitwell & Reepham Station is only the first phase of the group's ambitions. Phase two will consist of the reconstruction of 7 miles (11km) of track along the original formation to reach Reepham railway station, which though closed in 1959 like its neighbour, remains extant. Phase three, most excitingly, is to explore the possibility of the W&RR joining up with either the North Norfolk Railway or the Mid-Norfolk Railway, which would make for an impressive achievement for railway preservation in Norfolk.

Mid-Norfolk Railway

The Wymondham to Fakenham branch of the Norfolk Railway opened in 1849, forming a continuous line of railway from Wells-next-the-Sea in the north to Wymondham in the south of the county. Like its northern section, over which now runs the Wells & Walsingham Light Railway described above, the Wymondham–Fakenham line saw dwindling traffic returns in the 1960s, its passenger trains being replaced by the cheaper DMUs before the inevitable withdrawal of passenger services in 1969. Like the neighbouring W&WLR, freight continued to

Wymondham station on the MNR.

be carried over the route, albeit on an increasingly sporadic basis, until 1989 when the line closed completely.

Plans to preserve the line had begun to take shape even before its closure: an enthusiasts' group, the Fakenham & Dereham Railway Society, was formed in 1978, their goal being to maintain and extend the line as well as to run a service on it. They started by leasing Hardingham station, and created a small museum and heritage centre there; however, the society was forced to move from the site in 1986, relocating temporarily at the station in Yaxham before taking on a long-term lease at County School station in 1987.

Announcement of the closure of the entire line followed soon after, prompting the formation of a new company called the Great Eastern Railway Company, intended to work closely with the F&DRS to secure the line for preservation.

The subsequent history of the relationship between the GERC and the F&DRS became for a time rather complicated and need not concern us here, but suffice to say that by 1994 access to the line had been granted by BR and restoration work by the society could commence. There were still problems regarding the tenancy of the land, but by 1998, after a rationalization of forces, the line was purchased outright by the newly formed Mid-Norfolk Railway Preservation Trust, making it secure for the future.

Now the MNR have $11\frac{1}{4}$ miles (18km) between Wymondham and Dereham, with a further 6 miles (9.6km) to the north not currently in regular use. Unusual amongst preserved railways, the Mid-Norfolk owns only two steam locomotives, the remainder of the roster comprising diesel-hydraulic locomotives and a comprehensive cross-section of historic DMUs, although the MNR frequently hosts guest steam locomotives from other preserved railways.

The MNR differs from other preserved lines in that it has always intended itself to be a 'community railway', with the intention of running commuter services alongside its preservation-led activities. Further to this, the line offers itself as a resource for training, both for main-line maintenance contractors and local rail franchise holder Greater Anglia, as well as for the fire, police and ambulance services, a role no doubt aided by the 'modern image' stock maintained by the railway.

A further development with which the MNR is involved is the proposed Norfolk Orbital Railway, a modern transport project that would see the MNR link up with the North Norfolk Railway; this has been described in further detail in Chapter 8.

Early days on the BVR. Romney, Hythe & Dymchurch locomotive Winston Churchill *is seen here on the turntable at Wroxham in the early 1990s.*

Bure Valley Railway

The Bure Valley Railway, a 9-mile (14.5km) long, 15in-gauge railway, is unusual not only for its size, but also its youth, having opened to the public as recently as 1990. It occupies part of the trackbed built by the East Norfolk Railway in 1877, but unlike many other heritage railways mentioned in this chapter, the standard-gauge line did not close until 1982 – although passenger traffic ceased in 1952, both coal traffic and transportation of construction materials meant that freight services continued for another thirty years.

The BVR runs between Aylsham and Wroxham, via what is now Norfolk's only operational rail tunnel, carrying the little trains under the Aylsham bypass where previously there had been a level crossing for the standard-gauge trains.

At the time the BVR opened, it was owned by a company called RKF leisure, which ran the line until 1991 when the parent company went into receivership. Broadland District Council, eager to retain the line and prevent the land being sold off for development, purchased the trackbed, ownership of which they retain to this day. The operation of the line is looked after by Bure Valley Railway Limited, a company formed in 1991 that runs the railway on a not-for-profit model with volunteer support, as is common with most other heritage lines.

In the early years of the line's operation, the BVR leased locomotives from the Romney, Hythe and Dymchurch Railway in Kent, a similar 15in-gauge line, but one with a much longer history. It was built in 1927 as a result of the joint efforts of two noted racing drivers (and railway enthusiasts) Captain John Howey and Count Louis Zbrowski. The author remembers riding the BVR as a child in around 1991–2, being hauled by the RH&DR's No. 9, *Winston Churchill* (built 1931) and the BVR's own No.1, *Wroxham Broad*.

This last is an intriguing locomotive. Strongly reminiscent of the locomotives built by the GWR for the 1ft 11½in-gauge Vale of Rheidol Railway, it was constructed in 1964 as a steam outline, petrol-hydraulic locomotive and named *Tracey-Jo*. Its career took it to the miniature railway at Fairbourne, as well as the RH&DR, and railways at Blenheim Palace, Lightwater Valley, Steamtown (Carnforth) and Kirklees, after which in 1991 it found a home, still in petrol-hydraulic form, at the BVR. A major rebuild then followed, resulting in the renamed locomotive returning to service in 1992 as a proper steam locomotive, in which form she has remained as a stalwart on the BVR.

The BVR now owns eight locomotives in total: three diesel locomotives – one of which, No. 3 *2nd Air Division USAAF* (a long name for a small locomotive), was built to assist in the construction of the line – and five steam locomotives, all of which, with the exception of *Wroxham Broad*, were built for, or by, the BVR.

Thanks to the close association with the Broadland District Council, a footpath runs in parallel with the line along its entire length, and the railway has impressive facilities at its headquarters at Aylsham; these were constructed from scratch in 1991 on the site of the original Aylsham station.

Mangapps Railway Museum

Burnham-on-Crouch in Essex is not perhaps a town with which one makes an immediate association with railways, although the line that serves it – built by the GER in 1889 – is still in service. Nonetheless, Burnham is the home of the Mangapps Railway Museum, a private collection in farmland that is owned and maintained by the Jolly family, and houses a large collection of locomotives, rolling stock and railway-related artefacts, both large and small, collected from East Anglia as well as further afield.

The museum incorporates an impressive yard and a small station – the station building being that from Laxfield on the Mid-Suffolk Light Railway – as well as a $^3/_4$ mile (1.2km) length of line for passenger traffic. Other restored buildings on site hail from other parts of the East Anglian system – the signal box, for example, was rescued from Haddiscoe Junction, and a M&GNJR waiting room was moved from Great Ormesby station.

The collection of locomotives represents both steam and internal combustion, examples of both being in working order, whilst other examples are undergoing restoration. Much of the locomotive stock is industrial in nature, although some of the i/c locomotives are of BR parentage, with the inclusion of some BR electric multiple units, and even Metro-Cammel stock from the Northern Line.

The 15in-gauge locomotive Spitfire on the Bure Valley Railway.

Bibliography

Adderson, R. and Kenworthy, G., *Branch Lines around Cromer* (Middleton Press, 1998).

Adderson, R. and Kenworthy, G., *Branch Lines around Wroxham* (Middleton Press, 2012).

Adderson, R. and Kenworthy, G., *Branch Lines to Felixstowe and Aldeburgh* (Middleton Press, 2003).

Adderson, R. and Kenworthy, G., *Ipswich to Saxmundham: Including the Branch Line to Framlingham* (Middleton Press, 2000).

Adderson, R. and Kenworthy, G., *Saxmundham to Yarmouth* (Middleton Press, 2001).

Adderson, R. and Kenworthy, G., *Tivetshall to Beccles: The Waveney Valley Line* (Middleton Press, 2004).

Allen, Cecil J., *The Great Eastern Railway* (Ian Allan, 1955).

Beaumont, Robert, *The Railway King: A Biography of George Hudson* (Review, 2002).

Body, G. and Eastleigh, R.L., *The East Anglian Railway* (Trans-Rail Publications, 1967).

Burton, Rosemary, *The East Suffolk Railway* (Colourways Press, 1988).

Clark, Ronald H., *A Short History of the Midland & Great Northern Joint Railway* (Goose & Son, 1967).

Course, Edwin, *Barking to Southend* (Middleton Press, 2002).

Darsley, Roger, *The Wissington Railway: A Fenland Enterprise* (Industrial Railway Society, 1984).

Dutt, William A., *Norfolk* (Methuen, 1919).

Engel, Matthew, *Eleven Minutes Late* (Pan, 2010).

Gale, John, *The Coming of the Railways to East Anglia* (Melrose Press, 2015).

Garrod, Trevor *et al*, *England's Most Easterly Railway* (Railway Development Society, 1997).

Gordon, D.I., *A Regional History of the Railways of Great Britain – Vol. 5 The Eastern Counties* (David & Charles, 1968).

Ingram, Andrew C., *Branch Lines around Wisbech* (Middleton Press, 1997).

Joby, R.S., *Eastern Counties Railway* (Marwood Publishing, 1996).

Joby, R.S., *Forgotten Railways – Vol. 7 East Anglia* (David & Charles, 1985).

Joby, R.S., *Regional Railway Handbooks – No.2: East Anglia* (David & Charles, 1987).

Mitchell, V., Smith, K. and Ingram, A.C., *Branch Line to Upwell* (Middleton Press, 1995).

Mitchell, Vic, *Branch Lines to Harwich and Hadleigh* (Middleton Press, 2011).

Mitchell, Vic, *Branch Lines to Sudbury* (Middleton Press, 2012).

Mitchell, Vic, *Shenfield to Ipswich* (Middleton Press, 2011).

Moffat, Hugh, *East Anglia's First Railways* (Terence Dalton Ltd, 1987).

Oppitz, Leslie, *Lost Railways of East Anglia* (Countryside Books, 1999).

Popplewell, Lawrence, *A Gazetteer of the Railway Contractors and Engineers of East Anglia 1840–1914* (Melledgen Press, 1982).

Rolt, L.T.C., *Railway Adventure* (Constable, 1953).

Rolt, L.T.C., *Red for Danger* (Bodley Head, 1955).

Rosling Bennett, Alfred, *The Chronicles of Boulton's Siding* (The Locomotive Publishing Co. (copyright Ian Allan), 1927).

Satchell, Max, *Navigable waterways and the economy of England and Wales, 1600–1835* (Cambridge Group for the History of Population and Social Structure, 2017).

Treloar, Peter, 'A Scattered Family – The Cornwall Mineral Railway's 0-6-0Ts' (article printed in the *Railway Archive*, issue 30, Lightmoor Press).

Index